Mecanoo

Pietro Valle

Mecanoo
Experimental Pragmatism

Cover
Philips Business Innovation Centre,
FiftyTwoDegrees Nijmegen (Netherlands).
Detail of the façade

Flaps
Houben House and Studio, Rotterdam
(Netherlands). Entrance front onto
the lake, at night

'De Citadel' / Alexanderkazerne, The Hague
(Netherlands). View of the brick shell

Editor
Luca Molinari

Design
Marcello Francone

Editing
Laura Guidetti

Layout
Paola Ranzini

Translations
Shanti Evans (from Italian into English),
Language Consulting Congressi, Milan

We would like to thank Mecanoo
for supplying the illustrative material,
Christian Richters for the photographs
and Elena Carlini for her help in images
and texts editing.

First published in Italy in 2007 by
Skira Editore S.p.A.
Palazzo Casati Stampa
Via Torino 61
20123 Milan
Italy
www.skira.net

Printed and bound in Italy. First edition

ISBN 10: 88-7624-655-X
ISBN 13: 978-88-7624-655-5

Distributed in North America by Rizzoli
International Publications, Inc., 300 Park
Avenue South, New York, NY 10010, USA.
Distributed elsewhere in the world by
Thames and Hudson Ltd., 181A High Holborn,
London WC1V 7QX, United Kingdom.

Contents

Introduction

The name *Mecanoo* is a combination of three different words, the British model construction kit *Meccano*, the neoplasticist pamphlet *Mecano* drawn up by Theo van Doesburg in 1922 and the motto *Ozoo*, adopted in 1984 by a group of students in Delft for their competition entry for a housing complex in the area of Rotterdam's former zoo. Thus the assemblage of miscellaneous parts, the exploration of modern language and an interest in urban settlements, three basic themes in Mecanoo's work, are already encapsulated in the studio's name. To these should be added the practice of immersing oneself in the contradictions of the real world symbolized by the figure of the diver, adopted as an emblem by the group right after it won the aforementioned competition. The complex on the Kruisplein, a sensitive modern insertion into a historic context, was the first in a series of successful projects that Mecanoo has carried out over the twenty years of existence. Francine Houben, Henk Döll, Roelf Steenhuis, Erick van Egeraat and Chris de Wejier, the founding members of the office, have based their professional practice on a pragmatic approach and on group collaboration, constructing a series of public housing complexes throughout the eighties that were characterized by original planning solutions. In the nineties, Mecanoo diversified its practice to comprise the design of public buildings and university complexes as well, and stepped up its involvement in the kind of urban planning that reflected the processes in the expansion of the Dutch 'artificial landscape.' Although the members of the office have changed (the only one of the founders to have remained is Francine Houben), the 'polycentric' approach to design, the commitment to realism in construction and the rejection of a coherent style for the buildings created by the studio are all still there. This indifference to 'recognizability' and an interest in 'open' experimentation have led Mecanoo to adopt different languages (first the Modern and then contemporary codes), which have been 'taken to pieces' and recontextualized to find out if they are able to come up with a functional response to diverse conditions. Thus Mecanoo has built up an extraordinary capacity for the critical verification of contemporary architecture outside of any predetermined stylistic features, showing a preference for the productive and relational aspects of buildings. So any analysis of their work has to avoid looking for fixed points and instead reconstruct the complex procedures that link eclectic linguistic experimentation and effectiveness in the real world. In fact the *continuity in diversity* that characterizes Mecanoo represents one of the most interesting efforts of resistance to the media-oriented consumption that is typical of contemporary architecture, proposing a critical research that is continually opening itself up to new problems instead of taking refuge in fixed formulas.

Successive Slidings of the Modern

Up until the mid-nineties, Mecanoo's work was perceived as a reinterpretation of the language of the Modern Movement, which was appropriated, 'dismantled' and placed in contemporary contexts. This label has stuck, with the result that in 2000 Bart Lootsma, in his book *SuperDutch: New Architecture in the Netherlands*, was still portraying Mecanoo Architecten as clear representatives of the post-modern practice of appropriation and manipulation of historical styles, stressing the studio's continuity with other examples of the recycling of Modernism, seen as a code now accepted by Dutch culture.[1] Lootsma and other critics like Hans Ibelings seem to waver between an almost neo-traditionalistic evaluation of the Delft practice (based on the effectiveness of its practical approach to construction, which is seen as consistent with the needs of the building market) and one which emphasizes its reference to cultural forms that originated in the eighties: forms which, according to these critics, have now been superseded by the experiments of the new 'supermodern' architects like MVRDV, UN Studio or even the latest phase of Rem Koolhaas's work.

This judgement, while it contains elements of truth, is oversimplified and needs to take account of Mecanoo's complex relations with Dutch architectural culture. There is no doubt, in fact, that the studio has deep roots in its native land and seems to reject a generic 'internationalization' of its own architecture.

In the Netherlands, a country in which planning has historically played a major part and where rational thinking of a functionalistic nature has had a strong influence on society, the goals of modernization have already been achieved in the eyes of many. In his 1995 monograph on Mecanoo, Kees Somer speaks of the language of the Modern Movement in architecture as 'the equivalent of Christianity in our culture'.[2] This 'shared' condition renders Modernism more ideologically flexible here than in other countries. In recent decades, in fact, the language of the Modern Movement in architecture has taken on different meanings in the Netherlands. The typical image of the Dutch Modern is one of a rigorous functionalism translated into abstract forms clearly derived from the experience of De Stijl and the functionalism of the Nieuwe Bouwen of the thirties (it suffices to mention the figures of J.J.P. Oud, Johannes Duiker and Mart Stam). Yet this version of a socially engaged and formally coherent avant-garde, originating in the twenties and thirties, renewed in the fifties and sixties by architects/theorists like Jaap Bakema and resuscitated in the eighties by the 'neo-modern' of OMA, is less all-embracing than might appear. Recent studies like those of the Crimson group of historians or Ibelings' *Dutch Architecture in the Twentieth Century* have revealed the existence of breaks, discontinuities and above all *other* types of modernity that run through the Dutch culture of the twentieth century as parallel currents.[3] In opposition to neoplastic-constructivist abstraction, we find in the first place an organic-expressionist tradition attentive to the urban context and to construction that originated with the Amsterdam School in the twenties and then developed into the mysticism of the Wendingen group and recent experiences like that of Ton Albers. Then there is a functionalism of empirical origin that characterized all the so-called neo-traditional architecture of the thirties and forties, usually in opposition to the avant-garde movements and distinguished by its commonsense approach to the organization of the spaces, without any concern for the creation of a coherent image (one thinks of a transitional figure like W.M. Dudok). This 'invisible' architecture also characterizes much of the post-war production of housing by architects like Willem van Tijen and constitutes, to a much greater extent than the manifestos of the avant-garde, the cultural background that led to the Modern being seen more as an attitude towards reality than a style. On the opposite front, we find the ideological appropriation of the Modern carried out by the structuralist architects of the Forum group (first of all Aldo van Eyck and Herman Hertzberger) who, in the sixties and seventies, projected their expectation of social participation and elaboration of an 'open form' capable of interpreting programmatic differences into a continuity with the historic avant-gardes. These different visions, historically determined or contemporary with better-known movements, considerably modify the original unitary perception of the Modern and expand it as a flexible container characterized by a fairly wide variation in theory. At the end of the seventies, when the members of Mecanoo completed their studies, a form of reassessment of the modern language as an autonomous code, functionally determined but not influenced by ideological interpretations, was underway. As far back as 1963 the exhibition *Autonomous Architecture*, organized by Jaap Bakema, foreshadowed a historical architectural culture that looked back to examples from different periods and was capable of carrying out a comparative analysis of them. This search for spatially determined solutions that could be found in recent history led to the courses of 'Design Analysis' at the Delft University of Technology in the seventies that were to have such a powerful influence on the approach taken by Mecanoo.[4] In reaction to a scene like the one in the seventies, in which architecture was reduced to a social service (the result of the impact of Forum's Structuralism at the administrative level), theorists like Max Risselada rediscovered the autonomy of the modern project. Risselada, a professor at the Delft University of Technology, had his students examine the canonical examples of the twentieth century, 'break them down' into their components (spatial and typological units) and then 'reassemble' them in different contexts of settlement in order to try to understand the modification of ideas that had moulded them in relation to specific 'situations.' The practice of dissection of architecture, the indifference to the definition of archetypal forms and the continual questioning of the capacity of architectural language strongly influenced Houben, Döll, Van Egeraat, Steinhuis and De Wejier, who all took Risselada's course (Van Egeraat was even his assistant). The rejection of the individuality of language was so great that Risselada went so far as to take a project by one of the students and give it to the others as a basic model to modify. In this method there was an encounter between the interest in the spatial/functional definition of linguistic elements and their modification in specific situations. Paradoxically, the attempt to make architecture independent of ideologies (like the social one of the seventies) led, at

Delft University of Technology, to a situation of continual transition of forms that never remained fixed (the exact opposite of the contemporary neo-rationalistic search for invariable typological forms). In this relativity, which owed a debt both to the 'silent' functionalism of neo-traditionalism and to constructivist codes, one of the aspects most emphasized by the course was that of the transition between spaces: circulation acquires an added value as an element of relation of the parts. In its exploration of the tradition of the Modern, the conjugation between urban experience and servant space was underlined. Examples of routes amplified to the point where they acquire a public value (as with Le Corbusier's *promenade architecturale* or the connective elements in the Smithsons' complexes of the sixties) were studied in an effort to find an interaction between space, public function and specific location.

The themes of the course of Design Analysis were transferred directly into the work of the early members of Mecanoo and developed in their later practice. In the first place we find the adoption of elements of modern language in a 'spurious' form: there was no interest in defining a coherent alphabet (as happened in the contemporary neo-constructivism of the early OMA), but a desire instead for a comparison between different codes. In addition to the purism of the twenties present in some residential projects, there were elements of the British neo-brutalism of the fifties and sixties (the interaction between fixed and interchangeable units in the Smithsons' housing estates obtained through extended circulation) and a predilection for complex material forms like the ones found in the work of Aalto (filtered, in this case, by a recent reinterpretation that has liberated him from organic ideology). Mecanoo's architecture undoubtedly took the form of a process of appropriation and recombination, but these were never ends in themselves and served instead to describe contemporary complexity. The buildings designed by Mecanoo were never unitary but were composed of different parts shaped by spatial events and material discontinuities. These breaks, derived from the procedure of disassembly and reassembly, served to define 'places' linked to the activities carried out in the building (with a sort of 'functionalism' that was more symbolic than real) and to its orientation on the site (always present and perceptible). With the evolution of their work, the architects of the Mecanoo office began to 'layer' these differences: the various 'places' were at once separated and united by the circulation (the kinetic aspect of space was always present) and by an 'accumulation' of materials that, as we shall see, tended more and more to 'thicken' the building consistency. In this evolution Mecanoo has adopted procedures of superimposition, of flow and of distortion of the building shells that more closely resemble contemporary practices. In their more recent structures we can find elements of Gehry's work (both that of the seventies and eighties in which the buildings were treated as composite installations and his latest approach), the notion of the slab as an inclined slope that overcomes the difference between servant and served spaces developed by OMA and the manipulation of forms present in Alvaro Siza's work (cited by Mecanoo as an example of indifference to styles[5]). These influences, in part direct, are nevertheless subject to a radical process of modification in the search for a more precise response to the individual theme of design. Recognizing an inevitable principle of contradiction at the root of every spatial configuration, Mecanoo has criticized the functional programme and refused to accept its passive location in separate units. Unlike Koolhaas and the MVRDV, who amplified functional contiguity, Mecanoo has remained faithful to the interaction between settings as a means of uncovering their diversity. So their architecture cannot be reduced to a diagram, nor to a neutral envelope (as in many examples of 'supermodernism'), but is continually 'interactive' at different levels: spatial, functional and social. Rejecting a unitary interpretation of their works, Mecanoo uses references adopted to suit each occasion without 'residing' in them. Thus what emerges is not a coherent image of the works but a condition of permanent 'uninhabitability' of languages. Yet this instability does not translate into a celebration of lightness, but into the presence of 'dense' and layered forms. The members of Mecanoo are too conscious of the 'physical' nature of dwelling and the social responsibility of planners. However, they seek to have the 'material consistency' of architecture coexist with the relativity of its definition. Hence their approach is apparently eclectic, but in reality pursues a strategy that entails keeping a distance from certainties (styles, languages, uses) while reasserting the material presence of spaces. In this there is undoubtedly an unprecedented encounter between manipulation of precedents and 'empiricism' inherited from an anti-stylistic functional tradition. But this operational tension cannot be analyzed solely as a combination of forms. Rather it has to be treated as a response to a commonly accepted way of tackling functional programmes.

Paradoxical Functionalism

The hallmark of the Dutch functional tradition of the twenties and thirties, that of the Die 8 en Opbouw group, was a profound graphic and volumetric characterization of the functional units, which were identified with recognizable forms: on the one hand there was the De Stijl tradition of plastic decomposition, on the other the influences (stronger than in other European nations) of Russian Constructivism, mediated by figures like Mart Stam and the magazine *ABC*. This tradition of geometric abstraction of the programme and its transformation into an icon was rediscovered at the end of the seventies by Rem Koolhaas and OMA, who started to use diagrams to tackle contemporary design themes. The neo-constructivist decomposition of the programme undoubtedly had an impact on a whole generation of architects who emerged at the beginning of the eighties (Wim Quist, Benthem & Crouwel, Frits van Dongen, Jo Coenen) as well as on Mecanoo, becoming a sort of 'lingua franca' for the recent Dutch school.[6] This analytic/synthetic method has also been adopted by Mecanoo, but the group places less of an accent on the abstract decomposition of volumes and is more concerned with making the most of the relations between the parts of the programme. Other considerations enter into this: in the first place there is a critique of zoning and the search for 'areas of overlap' between functions typical of the solutions of Dutch Structuralism in the sixties and seventies (the notion of 'threshold' and of spaces with an 'and/or' relationship in the research of Aldo van Eyck). In other cases, some of the attainments of Team 10 have been reinterpreted in an interactive key to create multiple relationships between the parts of the buildings: the widening of routes to turn them into 'urban streets' within buildings (present in the Smithsons' work as well as that of Van den Broek and Bakema), the creation of 'clusters' of emerging public functions and the vision of the building as a miniature city made up of fixed and flexible parts are all aspects employed both in housing projects (the 'complex' composition of the high-density elements at Oeverpad in Amsterdam and Rochussenstraat in Rotterdam) and in public ones (the role of the routes in the Faculty of Economics and Management at Utrecht). To these programmatic achievements of the Modern, Mecanoo adds 'ambiguous' elements of clearly post-modern derivation that lead to complex interpretations and multiple spaces. Although initially separate, the functions of the programme are not all expressed with the same emphasis in the phase of recomposition: while certain areas take on an independent value and have an expressive spatial envelope, others are incorporated into 'invisible' ensembles and masked behind layered façades or partitions that do not reveal the substance inside: thus the 'transparency' of clear modernist origin is replaced by a deliberate 'opacity.' In housing for example, Mecanoo alternates the revealing of the division of the apartments with a screening of parts of the façade where the windows form an abstract pattern of urban and public value that tell us nothing of what goes on inside. This dissimulation, which refers to some of Aalto's last solutions and the research carried out by Emile Aillaud in France for a number of large housing estates in the sixties, creates an alternation of concealment and revelation that invites people to explore the building. The invisible parts and the screens are also a legacy of the 'anti-expressive' functionalism present in the Dutch neo-traditionalism of the twentieth century. Mecanoo, at times, acknowledges some of its solutions, introducing apparently vernacular elements into the shells to give continuity to neutral or opaque parts of the programme (such as the brick walls in the Vondelparc housing complex at Utrecht, in the Isala College at Silvolde or in the National Heritage Museum at Arnhem, all solutions harking back to the architecture of the past and its reinterpretation in the Amsterdam School, in the neo-traditionalism of the forties and fifties and in a number of Aalto's designs like the holiday home at Muuratsalo).

Thus to the initial datum of the breakdown of the programme into discrete parts in order to create a composite and not homogeneous whole, are added different procedures that tend to give a complex reading of the organization of the programme:

- In the first place there is an 'incomplete' and asymmetrical recomposition of the parts that creates a clear orientation of the whole: not all the functions are made expressive and what is developed instead is a geography of recognizable places pre-eminent with respect to others that obliterate the zoning of separate functions.

- If there is a clash, this occurs between routes and zones of activity in such a way as to emphasize the role of the orientation of stairs, corridors, galleries and openings. There is always more than one route leading to the public zones and the contrast between different parts is mediated by the multiplicity of spatial orientations of the whole. Here Mecanoo proposes a notion of kinetic and temporal space that gradually discloses knowledge of the buildings.

- Some functions or spatial events of particular public significance are emphasized to the point where they almost take on symbolic connotations (examples of this are the cone or the blue wall of books in the library of the Delft University of Technology or the patios characterized by a variety of materials in the Faculty of Economics at Utrecht).

In this alternation of ways of organizing the programme, Mecanoo avoids two extremes: a forced fragmentation of the parts and their indifferent insertion in a 'neutral' shell. The expressivity of the materials and the tectonic elements undoubtedly plays an important part in the articulation of the spaces.

Building Research and Material Delight

As is clear from the foregoing description, the manipulations of programme and space always have a material interface. The members of Mecanoo say they have little interest in ideological formulations and are more inclined to explore the modes of translation of the design into built form. This attitude is at once pragmatic and experimental, as it never assumes that a work of architecture is finished with its design but, on the contrary, shows how the process of construction and the participation of the users play a dialectical role with regard to the convictions of the architect. The 'production' of architecture, the constraints of the programme, the limits of the budget, the interlocutors (be they clients, users or contractors), the materials and the site become part of a broader process that leads the members of Mecanoo to clear their mind solely through the process that culminates in the constructed building. There is nothing surprising about the fact that Francine Houben's book *Composition Contrast Complexity* (2001) is a diary of adventures in execution in which the strength of the architecture emerges from the synthesis of various specific conditions which are always carried forward into the constructed building. Nor is it surprising that Henk Döll cites the concept of 'reflection in action' (borrowed from the book *The Reflective Practice. How Professionals Think in Action* by Donald Schon, lecturer in urban studies at the MIT) and explains that the dialectical relationship with the production of architecture leads to an open-ended research that goes beyond the apparent certainties of the 'professional' codes.[7] If intervention in the real world becomes a stimulus to reflect on architecture, the autonomy of design research is outweighed by the breadth of the practical problems, which prompt a continual self-criticism of previously adopted solutions. For Mecanoo this does not signify a celebration of the empiricism of the 'case by case' approach nor a sublimation of construction as a value in itself, but the emergence of a critical practice that uses the whole range of possibilities offered by design, including the contradictions in the process of production of buildings.

In this difficult and contradictory research, Mecanoo has distinguished itself from many of the best-known international offices, which prefer to develop easily recognizable formulas of communication. Instead, Mecanoo seems to want to 'narrate' the real without coming to definitive conclusions. This narration, which plays such a large part in Houben's book, finds an appropriate interface in the handling of material, in a sort of 'delight in things' that the architect often links to the figures of Charles and Ray Eames, in whose work she senses a union of play and research that enjoys getting down to the contradictions of reality.[8] This playing around with materials and structures is also a hallmark of Mecanoo's creations: their buildings often exhibit a simultaneous presence of different tectonic forms, finishes and materials that act as a counterpoint to the spatial complexity. The Mecanoo's works of architecture are 'dense,' layered and, in some cases, deliberately 'heavy,' almost as if the intention were to reveal the substance of the architecture as an alternative value to its image. Thus research into materials becomes a means of identifying the parts of a building, and this takes place not out of a fondness for the craftsman's touch but in an intentional dialectic with the purely formal definition of the spaces. There is also a continual alternation between structural expression and pure facing in the treatment of walls, frames and finishes: this juggling of 'heavy' and 'light' led Annette Le Cuyer to include Mecanoo in her book *Radical Tectonics*, along with designers like Patkau Architects or Enric Miralles. In addition to the value of the individual constructions in themselves, which we will analyze in a separate chapter, it is necessary to remember that the material also has a more general communicative function. In the first place the office's involvement of users in the choice of finishes means that physicality becomes a collective form of definition of the architecture, independently of any ideology of participation. In addition, it has the value of a practical criticism of the industrialization of buildings. If contemporary building production is subdivided, bringing it back to an apparent unity is, for Mecanoo, a mystification. The Delft-based group prefers to adopt multiple structural solutions in the same building as well as to put industrialized components in 'alternative' positions to the ones in which they are usually placed. These procedures of dissemination and estrangement of adopted techniques compose a further account of contemporaneity and form a tactile landscape that, independently of the forms, adapts to the complex conditions of the city and the territory. The conceptual flexibility between these different dimensions has a parallel in the interest in the interaction between building and land, or rather, between building and landscape, as well as in a kinetic vision of territorial space.

From the Routes to Mobility

We have already mentioned how movement in public spaces is underlined in Mecanoo's buildings: routes are used as a means of reuniting the parts of a building, but they are also an element that breaks down the divisions of traditional zoning. It is interesting to note how this interactive notion of space has gradually been extended to the territorial scale. From the initial balcony facing onto the city in the Kruisplein complex in 1984 to the research into mobility in the last few years, there is a thread that runs through progressively more complex solutions. If the housing complexes took the characteristics of orientation of the urban street into consideration, transferring them into the spaces of relationship (the stairs and galleries of the studio's first residential buildings), in later projects the routes have evolved from a simple linear configuration to form differences of level in section that open up vistas within the building: examples include the disjunction of levels in the Isala College at Silvolde and the auditorium suspended above the underground exhibition area in the 'Canadaplein' Cultural Centre at Alkmaar. The joints created by these detachments are not only traversable but frequently offer multiple points of view onto the adjoining spaces and encourage discovery of the building. The next step was the creation of hybrid multipolar territories, of 'fields' in which various points of attraction and movement are placed. Seen as a whole, these cannot be interpreted either as linear routes or as static 'centres.' How else could the internal space of the library of the Delft University of Technology be seen if not as a landscape of contemporary presences? The Anglo-Saxon notion of 'landscape' as a place/route between different visual stimuli influences the choice of introducing multiple movements into buildings. The proliferation of ramps/galleries that run through the thematic patios in the Faculty of Economics and Management at Utrecht reflects a further tangency between material articulation and orientation in space, as if the routes had to continually traverse successive 'recognizable places' to be effective. This logic has also shaped the research into territorial mobility of recent years and the recognition of the role played by the car as a viewpoint in the perception of the landscape. In a nation of artificial land that modifies its settlements and nature with great nonchalance, the growth of new conurbations in the Ranstad region (between Amsterdam, Rotterdam and The Hague) is interpreted as a process of alternation of recognizable built places and pieces of nature along the big motorways. This articulation of the 'route' is opposed to the current sprawl, which creates an undifferentiated tunnel of diffuse settlements. If routes, materials and landscape work together to define a continuity in the lack of homogeneity, this means that movement has the role of creating places and values in space. However, the indication of some routes is temporary. It has no definitive value but serves to create successive platforms for spatial interpretation that always project further on. Mecanoo's buildings find their 'habitability' not in static and sheltered places but in points of the routes that can be appropriated by different people and that serve to recognize the spaces and open them up continually to an 'outside themselves.'

Project and Consumption: Resistance and Criticism
In comparison with the spectacular communicability of other contemporary Dutch studios, Mecanoo's projects seem more subdued: in them we find no definitive formal synthesis, no consistent code of representation, not even the accent on the constructive form that is present in the office's realizations. At times it seems as if Mecanoo has adopted languages developed by others, in its presentations as well as in its buildings, without bothering to conceal their origin. These choices, often confused with professional conformism, are deliberate. The project is an incomplete and mo-

bile prefiguration that is transformed during the process of its realization. It proposes figures but leaves their relations open so that the construction can explore different ways of developing them. Unlike other studios, Mecanoo does not seem to seek a close correspondence between plan and execution: the former cannot be encapsulated in a single representation, the latter does not have to adhere to a pre-established icon and on the contrary 'amuses' itself by transforming the figures developed in the initial phase into more complex structures. A paradigmatic example of appropriate 'figuration' and its 'alteration' during the process of construction is Mecanoo's collaboration with the illustrator/comic-strip writer Joos Swarte in the realization of the Toneelschuur Theatre complex in Haarlem. Swarte's cartoons were used as a starting-point for the development of the building, without any concern about attribution of the ideas. The project of architecture, deliberately left incomplete, passes through various phases both in the translation of the drawing into built form and in the presentation made of it after construction. This last offers multiple images and cannot be traced back to a single viewpoint (Houben's book is paradigmatic in this regard). The 'shift' in ideas and the choice of incomplete synthesis is not a negation of architecture's classic means of communication but its projection into a post-medium condition.[9] The architecture, recognized in its complexity, does not work in a single significant dimension but coexists in different fields, each of which offers a specific interpretation of a complex whole. Unable to offer a final synthesis individually, the representative forms establish a dialectical relationship with each other. The division between project and realization becomes relative; each of the means of expression is critical design and partial construction of (the) architecture. Yet the overcoming of the divisions between theory and construction through an incomplete but relational communication is innovative: the members of Mecanoo go beyond the role of mere constructors or 'designers who take possession of other people's designs' (as they have often been judged) with a practice of continual expansion of their ideas into different fields: the concepts themselves are never disassociated from the forms that express them (whether visual or material) but are deliberately 'compromised' by them. If the figures can be found in a constantly modified manner in the various phases of work, the architecture becomes a continuous process of research that always has something more to say because it is not tied down to a definitive form. This belittling of planning understood in the classic sense of prefiguration can also be seen as a criticism of some forms of communication present on the international scene, and the Dutch one in particular. The Netherlands are organized by pragmatic tradition as a gigantic functional platform in which everything, from the form of the territory to choices of social policy, is regarded as susceptible of rational planning. This mode of operation is translated into communicative forms of synthesis that entail a reduction to diagrams, numbers and graphic schemes. If there is an impact of modernization it is recognizable, in its most extreme form, precisely in this representative synthesis and in its direct translation into reality. In the last decade this rational model has been the butt of a fair amount of criticism, especially from architects and planners, owing to its indifference to any system of values, its forced public participation and its implicit subjection to the rules of the market, which are optimized but never criticized. The linearity of planning processes has been taken as a point of departure by studios like OMA and MVRDV for a criticism of planning itself through use of the codes employed in it (the reduction of functions to simplified diagrams). In other cases (as in Ibelings' aforementioned 'supermodernism') the indifference of the real-estate market is translated into 'neutral' structures enclosed in iconic shells that simply contain adjoining pieces of 'zoning' without relating them to each other. This emphasis on the manipulation of diagrams or on the management of contiguity (an element, this last, recognized by Koolhaas in American buildings ever since the time of *Delirious New York*) has been translated into an interesting formulation extraneous to the classical autonomy of traditional architectural styles. All this has opened up new dimensions in research and has had an extraordinary success in international architectural circles owing to the clarity and versatility of the new iconological codes adopted. Yet this formulation often conceals an astute reiteration of existing procedures and the lack of a critical position with regard to the 'extreme planning' that characterizes the Netherlands. While the statistical figures or the undistinguished shells offer a paradoxical view of the market, they do not attempt to change it but to carry out a sort of 'cosmetic treatment' that allows the architects to straddle its procedures: this is the charge that Roemer van Toorn has recently laid at the door of this architecture, which he has baptized 'Fresh Conservatism'.[10] In his view, these practices do not diverge from the traditional Dutch 'Polder Model' of rational planning. Moreover, these works of architecture undergo considerable reductions in their built form precisely because they are indifferent to the processes of material translation of ideas, proposing instead a simple 'reconstruction' of the design image without any tectonic research. In 1991 Rem Koolhaas, concluding his spell of teaching at Delft University of Technology, organized a conference called 'How Modern is Dutch Architecture.' On that occasion he accused the passive adoption of modernist language of being an enslavement to the functional model that dominated politics and the national market (Mecanoo, significantly, refused to take part in the conference). Today, over fifteen years later, Koolhaas's strong views, however innovative, do not seem to have changed the system of production of building and planning, perhaps because they are only an intelligent amplification of it. If these procedures have had an enormous success abroad it is because, in other countries, they do not have to deal with a system of rational planning as highly evolved as the Dutch one and thus appear more innovative. In this context, Mecanoo's practice of 'dispersion' can be seen as a form of resistance to the excessive 'diagrammatization' of architecture that has emerged in the Netherlands in recent years. In the first place, their field of action extends much further than mere rendering (unlike the aforementioned studios). On the one hand, this boosts a faith in planning that is undoubtedly deeply rooted in the Dutch tradition, but does not allow them to rely upon accepted formulas, preferring incompleteness as a critical strategy. The partial adoption of acquired languages (from techniques of representation to the forms of the Modern) is a way of simultaneously speaking a lingua franca and undermining the certainties within it. Mecanoo Architecten shun the consumption of images and the techniques of communication of the avant-gardes. This is because they have understood that the idea of continual innovation has been absorbed by the market and has become pure consumption of fleeting messages. If a great deal of recent Dutch architecture opportunistically proposes a perverse marriage between avant-garde, communication and media success, Mecanoo prefers to carry out considerable modifications while working in silence. Their pragmatism in pursuing this goal is wholly Dutch, and the results are visible over the long run: while other studios have realized perfunctory translations of their ideas which do not stand the test of time, Mecanoo go on erecting structures that are a great success with the public and in which they often find themselves intervening with later additions, creating new interpretations (see in this connection the extension to the housing estate of Groothandelsmarkt in The Hague, with the adjoining zone of Haagse Erf). In this, the Delft studio has developed a personal elaboration of the idea of permanence in architecture that avoids the extremes of the nostalgic affirmation of *firmitas* or the superficial haste of contemporaneity. Permanence implies a continual modification of physical space that accepts deviations and contradictions, transforming them into elements of research.

[1] Bart Lootsma, *Superdutch, New Architecture in the Netherlands*, Thames & Hudson, London 2000, p. 17.

[2] Kees Somer, *Mecanoo*, 010 Publishers, Rotterdam 1985, p. 5.

[3] See: Crimson, *Too Blessed to be Depressed, Crimson Architectural Historians 1994-2002*, NAi Publishers, Rotterdam 2002, and Hans Ibelings, *Supermodernism, Architecture in the Age of Globalization*, NAi Publishers, Rotterdam 2002.

[4] Kees Somer, op.cit., p. 7.

[5] Francine Houben/Mecanoo Architecten, *Compositie Contrast Complexiteit*, NAi Publishers, Rotterdam 2001. Published in English as: *Composition Contrast Complexity*, Birkhäuser, Basel-Boston-Berlin 2001, p. 7.

[6] Hans Ibelings, *Dutch Architecture in the Twentieth Century*, NAi Publishers, Rotterdam 1994, pp. 120–35.

[7] Annette Le Cuyer, *Mecanoo*, Michigan Architecture Papers, Ann Arbor 1999, pp. 15–20.

[8] Francine Houben/Mecanoo Architecten, op. cit., p. 10.

[9] On this subject see: Rosalind Krauss, *A Voyage on the North Sea, Art in the Age of the Post-Medium Condition*, Thames & Hudson, London 1999.

[10] Hans Ibelings, *The Artificial Landscape, Contemporary Architecture, Urbanism and Landscape Architecture in the Netherlands*, NAi Publishers, Rotterdam 2002. It contains a series of critical essays, including: Roemer van Toorn, 'Fresh Conservatism and Beyond,' pp. 266–268 (originally published in *Archis*, 11, 1997).

Courthouse, Cordoba (Spain),
concept

Innovators in Housing

Housing represented Mecanoo's main field of activity throughout the eighties and has remained a constant exercise, alongside the design of public complexes, over the last decade as well. Experimenters in the area of social housing, the members of Mecanoo have introduced new elements on all three of the scales of the residential project: definition of the housing units, of the spaces of relationship within the housing complex and of the insertion of buildings into the urban context. Their continual output in this sector reflects the evolution of housing policy in the Netherlands and reacts to its problems with innovative designs. At the beginning of the eighties, when Mecanoo came onto the scene, Dutch residential development hinged on a district policy with small interventions of renovation in the existing city based on the participation of users and on rules that linked the size of the flats to family units. The group's early works reacted to this condition by inserting contemporary interventions into small- and medium-scale lots with variable density, routes on an urban scale and flexible accommodation intended for the young and for transient occupation. At the beginning of the nineties, the Fourth National Policy Document on Spatial Planning launched a major programme of expansion calling for entire new districts integrating housing development and extension of the suburbs with large estates called Vinex locations (after the acronym of the title of the supplement to the aforesaid document). The Dutch housing policy of the last decade can be divided up into an initial public boost for the planning of residential districts and then, from the mid-nineties on, a gradual delegation of the responsibility for public housing to private property developers. This change of direction is significant as planners now not only have to coordinate complex developments over time but render them attractive to different segments of the market.[1] In this phase too, Mecanoo excelled in the planning of entire public housing estates (such as Hillekop in Rotterdam) in both urban and suburban locations. In these, we find processes of development in phases (to support policies of growth that can be absorbed by the market), an original mixture of types that break down the homogeneity of interpretation of 'planned' districts (overcoming the dichotomy between 'high' and 'low' density), an attentive policy of public spaces of relationship and aggregations of dwellings open to various uses.

Houben House and Studio, Rotterdam (Netherlands). Garden front

An analysis of Mecanoo's collective residential projects can be divided up on the basis of the three scales of intervention, that of the general layout on an urban scale, that of the spaces of relationship between the housing units and that of the dwelling itself, since the Delft-based studio's contribution in each of them has been significant.

A first element that emerges in the overall design right from the early small-scale insertions in Rotterdam (Kruisplein, Bospolder and Tussendijken)

is that of heterogeneity, with the presence of different densities within the same complex. This strategy attained a first goal in the Hillekop complex, where linear buildings served by common stairs (three/four storeys high) co-exist with an eighteen-storey-high fan-shaped tower (echoing Aalto's scheme for the Neue Wahr building in Bremen) and terraced houses. The whole forms a composite set of public and semi-private spaces that traverse the structures with roads, footpaths and plazas.

Mecanoo uses leaps in scale to break down the homogeneity of the 'fixed density' of classical housing estates and to create a piece of city with recognizable 'places' characterized by the alternation between outstanding features and continuity. This strategy is also used to handle programmes of social housing with minimal accommodation in a frank and straightforward manner: it is not the masking of the façade with 'urban' elements that generates quality of place (as in the parallel 'critical reconstruction' of the European city that was all the rage in the eighties with the IBA and the proposals of the Krier brothers), but the articulation of modern language, with an accent on its ability to handle the whole range of scales of settlement. This attitude, already discernible in the initial Hillekop project in Rotterdam, attained fuller expression in the Groothandelsmarkt public complex in The Hague (which comprises an eleven-storey 'lighthouse,' a seven-storey 'ship' and a 'sea' of two-storey terraced houses) and in the more sophisticated Vondelparc in Utrecht. Here a green belt (a sort of semi-public common) connects a three-storey linear brick building with common stairs, a series of courtyards that enclose terraced duplex flats and a group of five-storey blocks of flats. The variety of urban places that these different typologies create is amplified by the use of materials that mark the alternation between exteriors in brick (facing onto the green corridor) and interiors in white plaster (the courtyards). The private spaces are then connected with the outside through windows in the walls of the courtyards and cuts in the fronts or on the corners of the blocks of flats that indicate different urban places.

The insertion of the 'themed' landscape element into residential complexes is another of Mecanoo's achievements: the public and semi-private spaces are treated not in the traditional manner (courtyard/street) but with diversified finishes that help to characterize different places within repetitive structure of the housing. The use of greenery as an 'artificial' element first appeared in the Ringvaartplasbuurt Oost complex at Prinsenland, a development in the suburbs of Rotterdam where Mecanoo organized bands of different linear elements (terraced houses and buildings with shared staircases), arranging them in a zigzag pattern and interspersing them with four 'themed landscapes': French (formal geometric), English (picturesque), Japanese (Zen) and Dutch (farmyard). This initial schematization was developed in later complexes, attaining more integrated solutions in projects like the Rijksvoord district in Arnhem where the organization of 'bands of landscape' supports various buildings that can be erected in phases, maintaining a complete identity at each stage.

The organization of circulation follows this enhancement of common spaces and Mecanoo Architecten have been particularly careful to coordinate the presence of the car in housing complexes while maintaining a substantial presence of pedestrian areas. The invention of a dual level of access to the residences tried out in the Nieuw Terbregge complex in Rotterdam is exemplary of this: a lower road providing access to the garages is interpolated with flower beds in which grow trees that reach up to the higher public wooden 'deck' for pedestrians. This in turn allows light through to the level for vehicles through the joints between the planks and the holes through which the trees grow. The two types of routes are separate, but also united by the landscape, the light and the surface of the horizontal screen. As we have seen, the materials, although associated with individual buildings, play an important role of identification on the urban scale. Mecanoo employs different finishes to mark the various places but also 'layers' parts of the façade to disguise the repetition of the apartments. Exemplary, in this sense, is the Herdenkingsplein intervention in Maastricht, where Mecanoo had to define the backdrop of a large urban court in which other buildings were present (including the Art Academy designed by Wiel Arets). Houben and her partners designed a four-storey building that fronts onto the square with a slender full-height colonnade that alternatively screens portions of balconies (set here as a visible element of opening onto the city) and hanging wooden screens that make the position of the flats completely invisible to the outside observer. The diversified use of the frame, balconies and screens creates different impressions of the depth of the building, which articulates the urban scale by referring it by turns to the colonnade, the horizontal bands of the galleries and the mask of the suspended wooden screens.

The balconies at Maastricht, placed between the colonnade, the façade and the wooden screens, are an element of relationship between the dwelling, the building and the city. We have already spoken of the attention paid by Mecanoo to circulation as a definer of places. In the block of flats, common staircases and balconies create multiple links between street, building and apartment, often presenting themselves as elements 'detached' from the main building block, almost as if they were stage catwalks facing onto different scenes. If this is what happened in the early experimental housing of the eighties, Mecanoo later employed mixed elements to serve the apartments in the same building in such a way as to divide them up into micro-communities. The 'ship' at the Groothandelsmarkt, for example, mixes portions of building served by common stairs and sections with shared galleries.

The recent Oeverpad block of flats in Amsterdam is a sort of 'summation' of the interaction of different parts, routes and materials put into effect by Mecanoo in housing to create recognizable places within a serial construction. A complex with a square courtyard is open on one side to give all the apartments a view of the nearby Sloterplas Lake, and is treated as a vertical assembly of two wings of five floors faced with a curtain wall superimposed on a four-storey brick base that connects up with the surrounding buildings. The constructivist play of volumes alternates with that of the facings, which create a contrast between the outside and inside of the courtyard as well as different 'layers' of a single façade. While the street fronts are monolithic walls with individual windows piercing the brick face, the interior of the courtyard is characterized by 'curtains' of perforated sheet metal that screen the balconies, behind which the flats are faced with wooden panels as at the Herdenkingsplein. Even the ground is layered and a deck at the mezzanine level covers the car park and faces onto a garden with trees at the centre of the courtyard. Access to the apartments is provided by galleries served by common staircases, which become a sort of 'elevated road' that traverses the geography of the different materials used to characterize the courtyard, with significant points of view onto the city and the lake.

In the low-density aggregations it is the spaces adjoining the building that act as a territory of mediation between public and individual dimension. The boundaries between these areas are mutable and often produced by the modification of acquired typologies. In the Park Haagseweg complex in Amsterdam, Mecanoo staggered the units of a row of duplex apartments, forming a series of semi-open patios shared by three flats, and succeeded in breaking down the traditional impression of identical homes set side by side. In the Rijkswoerd at Arnhem and at Nieuw Terbregge they invented a new aggregation of 'eight dwellings under the same roof,' designing a cluster of homes with individual entrances that form a sort of large villa: here too the opposition between individual and collective has been overcome by the invention of a new building type. These low-density solutions are also responses to the growing preference of the market for the detached house: Mecanoo Architecten have shown how simple forms of aggregation can provide an alternative to suburban individualism while maintaining a percentage of communal space.

On the scale of the apartment and the single dwelling, Mecanoo has been in the vanguard ever since the Kruisplein, devoting itself to solutions not intended for the traditional model of the family and offering flexible schemes that take into consideration the emergence of a mixed range of users. Francine Houben's house in Rotterdam is more a prototype for layouts of the collective residence than a house for a single family. It has at least three or four alternative routes linking the various rooms, with a continual reiteration between the zones of use without there being a servant space separated from the served one. The interior is influenced by Loos's Raumplan and the purist schemes of Le Corbusier (where there is always a ramp and a staircase, offering two speeds of crossing of the same spaces). Yet it offers a quality of settings completely different from those examples. Just as this is a 'house made up of various houses,' the flats of community housing are subdivided into various levels of freedom. In the first apartments designed in the eighties, Mecanoo Architecten always included an 'open' part that could be subdivided at will (it is an entire bay in the single-level flats or one of the two levels in the duplex ones). Later, they developed two ways of traversing domestic space: in the apartments of the multifunctional complex in the Oude Torenstraat in Utrecht there is a central access space that serves the rooms but, at the same time, all the partition walls are interrupted before the outer shell, leaving external openings with sliding doors that link the rooms two by two. So it is possible to move both from the centre and in a ring, as well as to organize subgroups of rooms equidistant from the service areas (bathroom and kitchen) that can be united and separated to accommodate a variety of groups.

The creation of micro-communities that coexist in the same housing also concerns the different uses that can be made of it, with the allocation of a room or a level as a study area, developing the theme of home working. The interesting aspect of this research is the tension between the apparent normality of the dwellings and their flexibility obtained through a careful organization of standard units linked in an alternative way. In this research, the architects of Mecanoo establish a connection between examples derived from the past and from the present: in the 'flexible' dwellings they reinterpret the eighteenth-century Dutch townhouse with its parallel movements between rooms in enfilade and access corridor, the mediaeval house-shop and the experimental solutions for collective housing developed at the Vkhutemas, in Russia, in the twenties. The differences between bourgeois and working-class space or between public and private are overcome in the interest of an increased recognizability of the spaces of the house.

[1] Arjen Oosterman, *Housing in the Netherlands, Exemplary Architecture in the Nineties*, NAi Publishers, Rotterdam 1996, pp. 9–29.

Vondelparc
Utrecht (Netherlands)

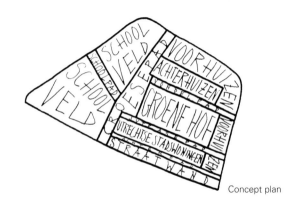

Programme: Urban planning
for 19,600 sq.m of public space
and design of 203 housing units
Design: 1998–99
Execution: 2000–02

Concept plan

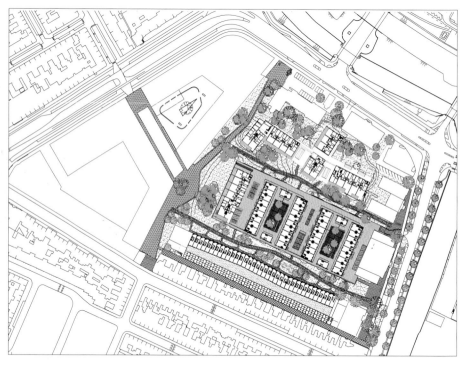

Site plan

Window in the enclosure
of a courtyard

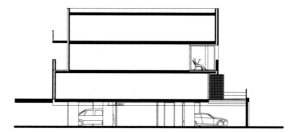

Courtyards, section

Courtyards, second floor

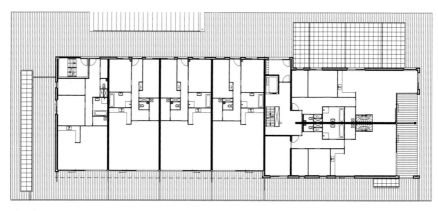

Courtyards, first floor

Blocks of flats on the park, ground floor

Green belt

The interior of a courtyard
with the terraces
of duplex flats

Linear building

Ringvaartplasbuurt Oost
Rotterdam (Netherlands)

Programme: Urban plan for the
residential development of an area
of 10 hectares with 550 dwellings
Design: 1988–91
Execution: 1991–93

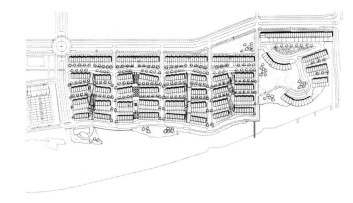

Development plan

Triplex flat in the terraces

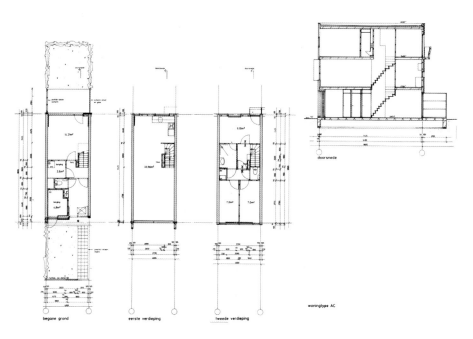

The terraces seen
from the opposite shore
of the lake

Standard duplex flat
in the terraces

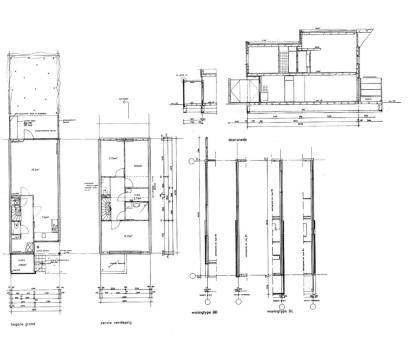

doorsnede

begane grond

eerste verdieping

woningtype BB

woningtype BC

End of the ship
and terraces

English garden between
the terraces

Ends of the terraces
with two materials on the
fronts

Herdenkingsplein
Maastricht (Netherlands)

Programme: 52 housing units
and a square in the historic centre
of Maastricht
Design: 1990–92
Execution: 1993–94

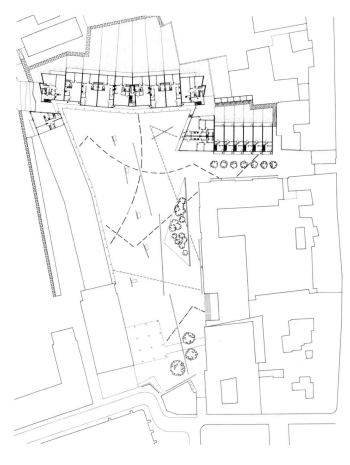

Site plan

Entrance to the courtyard

View of the courtyard

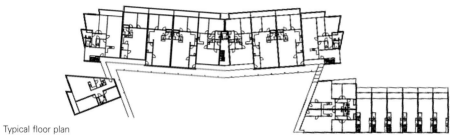

Typical floor plan

Nieuw Terbregge
Rotterdam (Netherlands)

Programme: Urban plan for 107
'double-deckers' and 48 waterfront
houses for a total floor area
of 24,655 sq.m
Design: 1998
Execution: 1999–2001

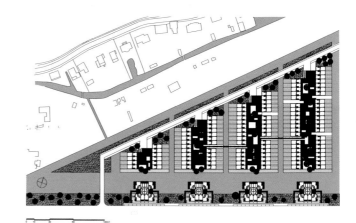

Site plan at the level
of the courtyards

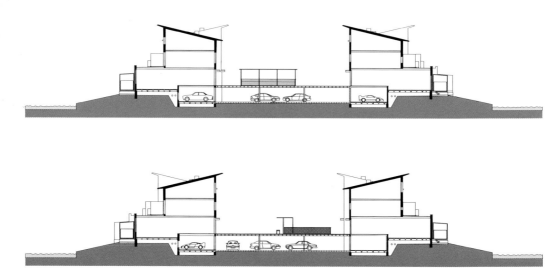

Cross-sections
of the canals-terraces-
courtyards-deck system

Prospect of the terraces
onto the courtyards

Courtyard with deck

Vehicle entrance to the
courtyards under the deck

Buildings with eight flats
on the canal

Oeverpad
Amsterdam (Netherlands)

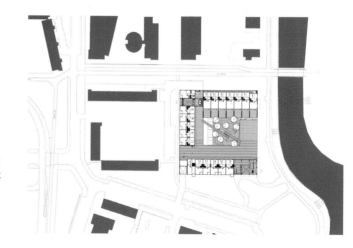

Programme: Residential building
with 120 apartments of sizes varying
from 104 to 168 sq.m covering a total
floor area of 20,000 sq.m and car park
Design: 2002–03
Execution: 2003–05

North-west corner

Montage of the curtain-wall
on the brick base

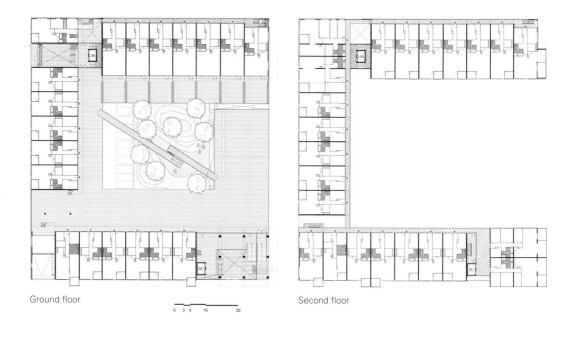

Ground floor

Second floor

0 3 5   10   20

Interior of the courtyard
with balconies and screens
in micropore sheet metal

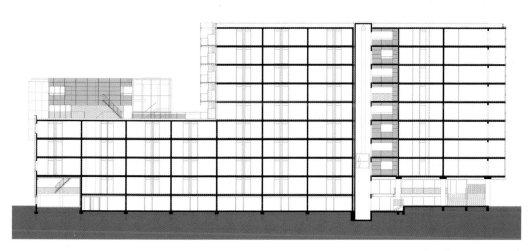

Section through
the south block

Prospect of the courtyard
onto the lake

Houben House and Studio
Rotterdam (Netherlands)

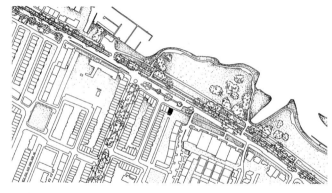

Programme: House with studio
of 300 sq.m
Design: 1989–90
Execution: 1990–91

Site plan

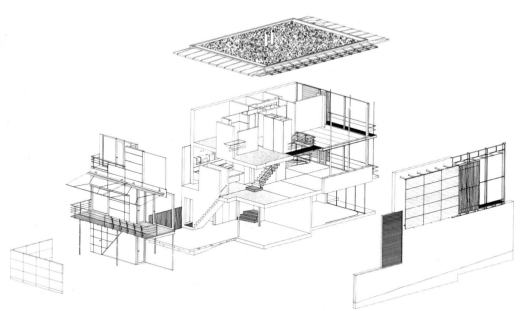

Exploded axonometric
drawing

Entrance front onto
the lake, at night

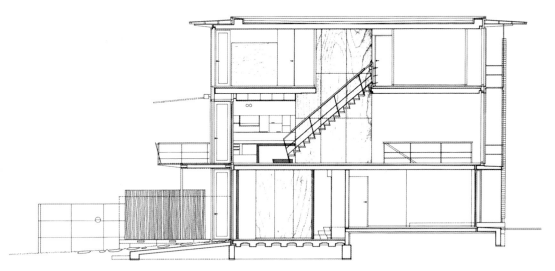

Longitudinal section

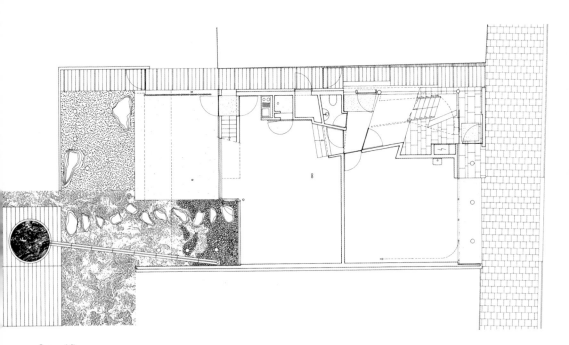

Ground floor

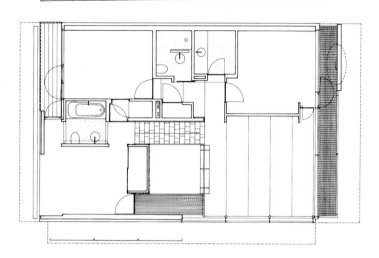

Second floor

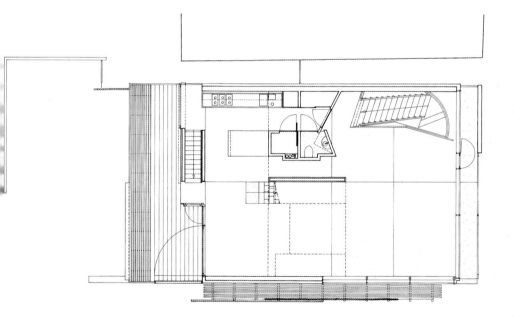

First floor

Interior, first floor

Interior, second floor

Hybrid Buildings, Coexistence of Functions

The procedures of disassembly of the program into parts and articulation of circulation have found application not just in many of the public complexes designed by Mecanoo but also in specific 'hybrid buildings' that house multifunctional programmes. Here different situations exist side by side and the spatial organization has to alternately connect the parts and leave them independent. Mecanoo Architecten have often found themselves handling this type of programme and have been inspired by the challenge of new aggregations to come up with some of their most original solutions. The modern Dutch tradition, attentive to the organization of programmes, has developed various approaches in the field of multipurpose buildings which have often rejected the division into parts typical of functionalistic zoning.[1] To put it very briefly, we can identify three directions:

– The horizontal and vertical stratification of functions within the same complex with their spatial interaction in section and in the tectonic organization. An example of this is Johannes Duiker and Bernard Bijovet's Gooiland Hotel complex at Hilversum of 1935, where the three-dimensional manipulation of planimetric figures and vertical cuts creates multiple overlaps between a commercial ground floor, a hotel with a raised plaza on the upper level and a theatre at the back.

– The interest in 'introverted' spatial configurations like the casbah shown by the Structuralism of the sixties (and by Herman Hertzberger in particular), with the creation of tectonic grids and routes that can be colonized by different functions, which are inserted in a dense urban fabric opening onto 'inward-looking' public spaces.

– The management of the 'contiguity' of different functions which are alternatively enclosed in an all-embracing container or laid out along a route/dynamic flow, both proposed by Rem Koolhaas with his 'urban congestion' or, in his more recent works, with the invention of inclined functional platforms that unite zones of use and circulation.[2]

The members of Mecanoo have reinterpreted these modalities in a personal manner without espousing the messages associated with them (in fact they steer clear of both Hertzberger's ideology of the 'community' and Koolhaas's conception of 'parcelling'). As with other single stylistic elements adopted and then radically modified, these three forms of relationship have been employed to obtain a complex coexistence of independence and interaction between the parts.

The fact that Mecanoo Architecten do not seek personal solutions but explore the legacy of the Modern and the contemporary leads them to view the solutions acquired in a dialectical manner. Between the extremes of total fragmentation (as in Deconstructivism) or the packing of complex pro-

Faculty of Economics and Management, Utrecht University, Utrecht (Netherlands). The glass front and the lobby with the suspended auditoria

grammes into an undistinguished *decorated shed*, they choose intermediate options that cannot be fitted into a defined scheme.

Continuing the experimentation undertaken in a number of high-density housing developments with various servant spaces, Mecanoo tried out the inclusion of different functions in a multi-storey linear building in the Rochussenstraat complex in Rotterdam. Flats, studios for artists, offices, a residence for a foundation and a police station are laid on top of one another along the longitudinal section of the same block. In its depth, Mecanoo has succeeded in placing spaces opening on only one side with a gallery and rooms that open on two sides with a central corridor. The façades have several levels of openings, alternating faced surfaces and exposure of the structural framework. Halfway between a unified container of different parts and a layered structure, Rochussenstraat is an example of intelligent urban insertion that 'slows down' the discovery of its complexity by disclosing its parts gradually.

The complex of Oude Torenstraat at Hilversum breaks down the compact stratification of Rochussenstraat and rearranges it in several adjoining blocks that house different functions and display gradations of privacy in the passage from the existing street to the inner courtyard and then all the way to a zone of parkland at the back. A curved façade clad in copper contains offices and is suspended above a base of pilotis onto which open the commercial spaces that characterize the public street front. From this urban 'backbone' run two orthogonal wings with apartments served by galleries. They are screened with wooden porches that open onto an inner courtyard with a deck (the whole of the space inside is faced with wood and 'warm' in appearance). The exteriors on the other hand see the main fronts of the flats treated as a curtain-wall of glass and metal, which faces onto an existing park containing a small existing cemetery. With the alternation of the materials, the density of openings and the progressive transparency, Mecanoo has been able to articulate a sequence of urban locations (street, courtyard, garden), binding them together through the architecture of the building.

The assemblage of urban sections that at once intersect with and emerge from one another is found again in vertical form in the Montevideo tower at the Kop van Zuid docks in Rotterdam. A hotel, offices, a sports centre and various types of apartment are located by turns in various parallelepipeds and then 'extracted' vertically in such a way as to form a complex urban base (like a piece of city made up of various buildings) from which the tower rises at the end. Mixing concrete and steel structures, this project refers to two Koolhaasian precedents, bringing them together: the section of the Manhattan Club with the insertion of multiple functions in the same block and the 1983 project for the town hall of The Hague, in which a single function is split up instead into several adjacent towers. Skilfully blending these two references (both derived from the skyscrapers of Raymond Hood), Mecanoo has eliminated their apparent opposition and accentuated instead the alternation of different fronts onto the city (terraces, projections, screenings). Rather than a shell, Montevideo takes the form of a vertical urban settlement that sets out to construct various scales of interpretation of the context with a single building.

It is interesting to compare this project with the recent Lange Jan and Lange Lies one for Heerlen. This is a curious double tower made up of two oblique blocks that lean towards and support each other in precarious equilibrium: the transfer of the functions from different shells into a single container creates a pulsating plan where two groups of dwellings are linked and separated in turns by the circulation core.

The contiguity of different functions emerges in the 'Canadaplein' Cultural Centre at Alkmaar, created partially by the enlargement of pre-existing structures: a library, museum, dance school and theatre appear to be separated by precise planimetric barriers and held together solely by a slender shell of wooden screens. The museum section, however, has the exhibition space interact with an auditorium, leaving spatial joints open and using the latter as a suspended volume with a sculptural solution that recalls the entrance of Hans Scharoun's Philharmonie. Curiously, this dynamic section is combined with a neutral zoning, proposing a disparity between the apparent minimalism of the urban image and the internal *tour de force*.

A neutral container screening a complex interior is found again, but with greater freedom than in the Canadaplein centre, in the project for Novartis: a parallelepiped set on the campus of the Swiss pharmaceutical company in Basel and containing a scientific centre with laboratories and an auditorium. The different parts are treated as 'incisions' that cut into the volume and face onto two internal atria located on different levels. The functions seem to rotate like suspended planes around the central voids, creating a multiplicity of views and articulating the 'introverted' distribution of the building. The outer of wooden screen alternately conceals and reveals the interiors, forming an ambiguous boundary to the whole complex. The laboratories are conceived as mobile units that can be transferred to different places (using the concept of 'hotelling' of work units) and accentuate the idea of dynamic scattering of the spaces around the atria. Hence the latter take on an almost Piranesian flavour with the dynamic projection of the volumes into the internal empty space.

The Faculty of Economics and Management at the Uithof in Utrecht returns to the metaphor of the casbah, organizing the spaces around three internal patios treated with independent landscaping themes (Jungle, Zen and Water). However, the repetition of minimal units, typical of structuralism, is completely obliterated by a variety of internal landscapes and by the hypertrophy of the routes (with oblique ramps in all directions) that turn the whole interior into a sort of theme park that proposes a series of 'journeys'.[3] The building facing onto the campus opposes the transparency of its curtain-wall to the opacity of the three auditoria that jut out into the double-height space of the entrance. Thus the 'introverted' explanation of the building is misleading: Mecanoo has shown there is much more relativity behind the formulas than appears: the casbah of structuralism has turned into an exotic journey, the internal street into a flying carpet.

The glazed atrium reappears as an element of cohesion in the aforementioned Toneelschuur Theatre complex at Haarlem designed in collaboration with Joos Swarte. Situated in a narrow mediaeval street lined with historic terraced houses, the complex treats the envelopes of the theatre halls as an assemblage of 'houses' finished with different materials, in a procedure that is reminiscent of the buildings/city of Frank O. Gehry's designs in the seventies and eighties. The main hall that projects into the street, supported by a single slanting pillar, is striking. The foyer hollows out a completely glassed-in covered plaza in the narrow corridor of the street. A staircase with galleries at different levels offers a panorama of the houses in front, involving them in the disposition of masses of the theatres. Passers-by can see the various levels of the foyer and are visible to the audience, establishing a collective dialogue through the glass wall/screen. Adopting a strategy diametrically opposite to the one at Canadaplein, Toneelschuur projects the complexity of its interior into the street and then tones things down in the theatres. These are functional containers painted completely black, efficient machines with movable partitions that avoid any spatial identity, focusing attention on the space of the stage and not on the shell.

We again find the alternation between transparency and layering of the building envelope, with its breakage by the routes to mark significant public places, in the competition project for the Città della Moda in Milan. A large cubic volume, located in the gardens of Porta Garibaldi, contains a school on the lower levels and a museum on the upper ones. At the intersection of the two parts, the cube is open in section and contains a multifunctional glassed-in space for fashion shows, served from the park by a large escalator that extends the idea of public catwalk to the outside. The whole of the rest of the envelope is covered with a motif of changing silhouettes that layer it with translucent 'skins,' reiterating the notion of clothing/decoration as a 'movable' image of the building.

Containers, collage, contiguity, layering, urban fabrics, landscapes and above all spectacular routes characterize these diverse projects. It is impossible to define a single spatial matrix for them, but this shows the versatility of Mecanoo, which does not lay down a fixed procedure for multifunctional programmes but handles them in different ways according to the circumstances.

[1] Hans Ibelings, *The Artificial Landscape, Contemporary Architecture, Urbanism and Landscape Architecture in the Netherlands*, NAi Publishers, Rotterdam 2002, pp. 104–35.

[2] Hans Ibelings, *Supermodernism, Architecture in the Age of Globalization*, NAi Publishers, Rotterdam 2002, p. 54.

[3] Francine Houben/Mecanoo Architecten, *Compositie Contrast Complexiteit*, NAi Publishers, Rotterdam 2001. Published in English as: *Composition Contrast Complexity*, Birkhäuser, Basel-Boston-Berlin 2001, pp. 80–81.

Laboratories and Research
Centre, Novartis Campus,
Basel (Switzerland). Central
atrium

Rochussenstraat
Rotterdam (Netherlands)

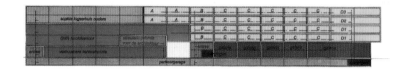

Longitudinal section with
organization of the parts

Programme: Multifunctional building
of 12,000 sq.m with offices, shops,
apartments and garage for parking
Design: 1991–92
Execution: 1993–95

Front onto Rochussenstraat

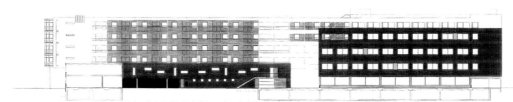

Elevations

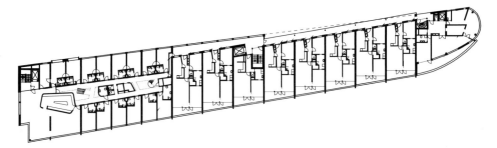

Third floor

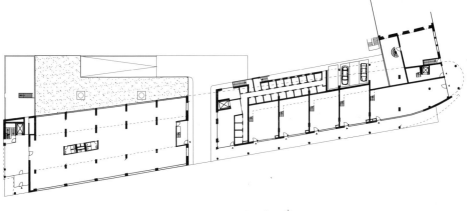

Ground floor

Urban front

Front onto the internal
courtyard

Oude Torenstraat Complex
Hilversum (Netherlands)

Programme: 18 apartments,
2,700 sq.m of offices and commercial
spaces and a garage for parking
in the city centre
Design: 1995–97
Execution: 1999–2000

Site plan

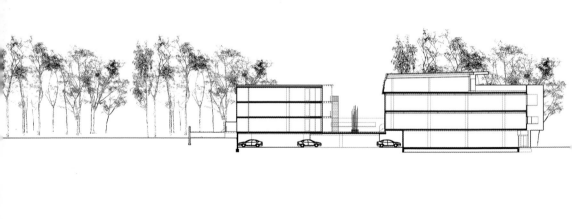

Cross-sections

Front onto Oude
Torenstraat

Glass front onto the park
with the cemetery

Entrance to the car parks
under the courtyard

Courtyard with deck

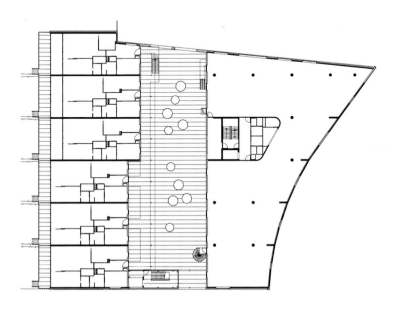

Plan at the level
of the courtyard

Montevideo
Rotterdam (Netherlands)

Programme: 153-m-high tower
with total floor area of 57,530 sq.m,
including 36,867 sq.m of apartments,
905 sq.m of pool, fitness and service
space, 6,129 sq.m of offices,
1,608 sq.m of shops and a garage
of 8,413 sq.m for parking
Design: 1999–2003
Execution: 2003–05

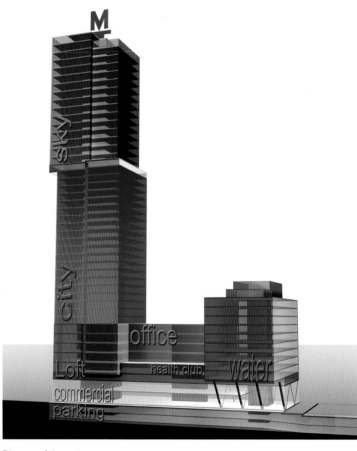

Diagram of the parts

View from south-east

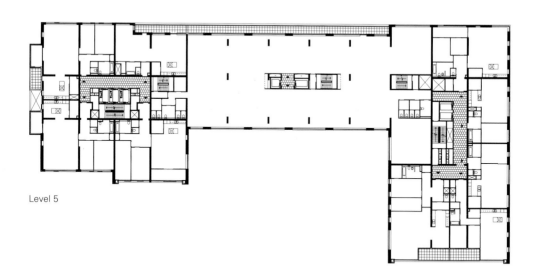

Level 5

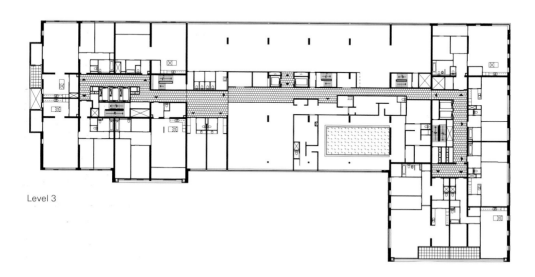

Level 3

Villa Montevideo,
apartments in the loft

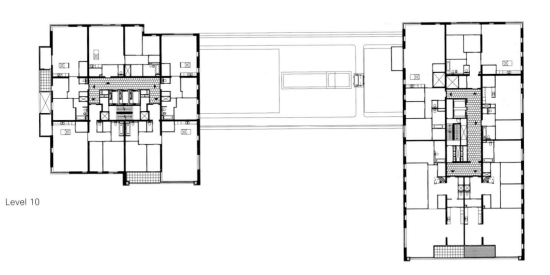

Level 10

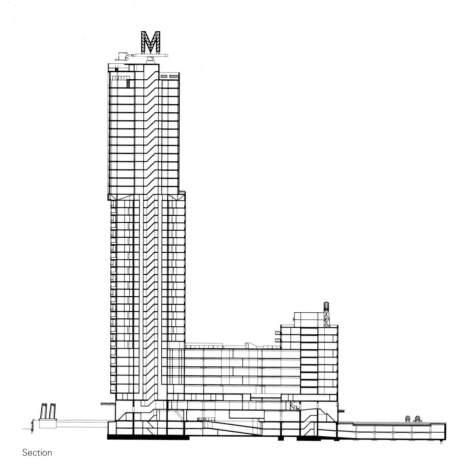

Section

Apartment in the loft

North front

Lange Jan and Lange Lies
Heerlen (Netherlands)

Urban skyline of Heerlen
with the towers inserted

Programme: Pair of residential towers,
each of 15,000 sq.m, with 31
and 25 floors respectively
and housing 110 apartments
Design: 2003–04

Concept

de torens zijn identiek

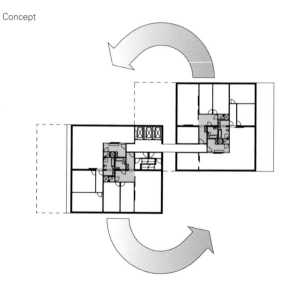

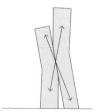
gelijke gedeelten in de torens

verplaatsing/ repetitie
van de plattegronden

stijgpunt & verloop van
de leidingschachten

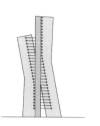
positie van de entrees

View from Muzelaan

View from Geerstraat

View from the square
in front of the theatre

'Canadaplein' Cultural Centre and Theater De Vest

Alkmaar (Netherlands)

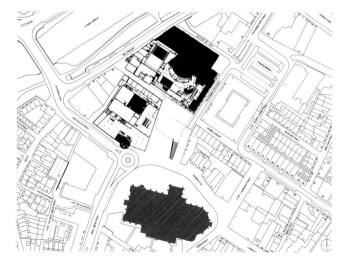

Site plan

Programme: Cultural centre of 9,300 sq.m with museum, library and music school. In the theatre: restoration of the foyer, small theatre, café and a 4.175 sq.m educational centre
Design: 1998–1999
Execution: 1999–2000

View of the entrance
to the library

Façade screened
with wood

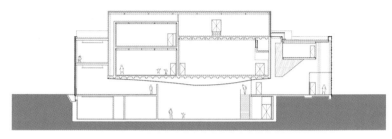

Section through the auditorium

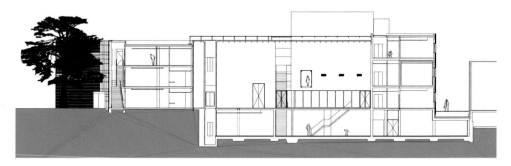

Section

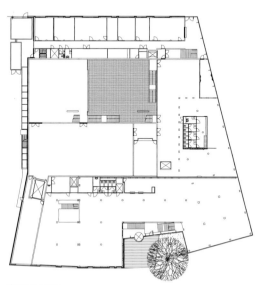

Ground floor

Second floor

Theater De Vest, foyer

Laboratories and Research Centre, Novartis Campus
Basel (Switzerland)

Programme: Innovative laboratory
and knowledge centre of 10,000 sq.m
Design: 2003

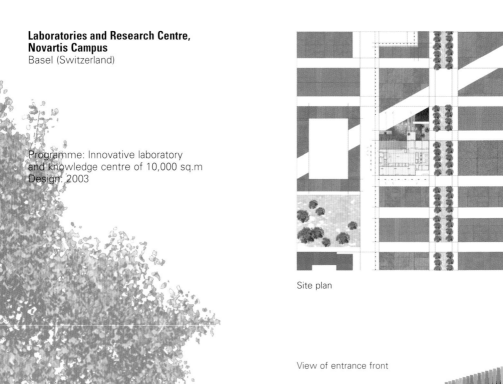

Site plan

View of entrance front

View of the model inserted
in the site

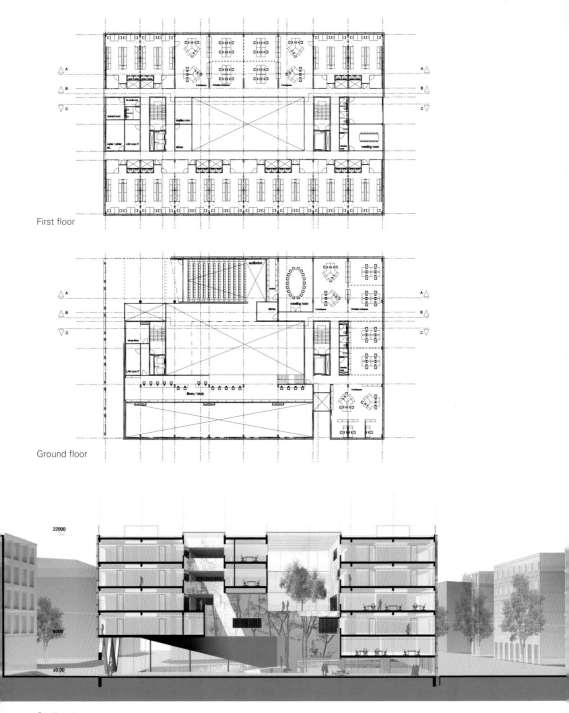

First floor

Ground floor

Section 1

View of the interior
from the lobby

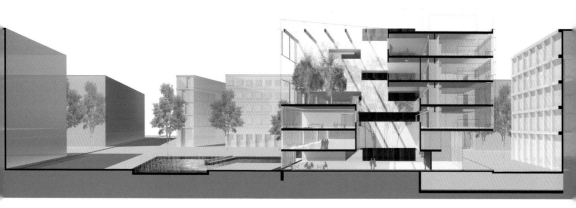

Section 2

Faculty of Economics and Management, Utrecht University
Utrecht (Netherlands)

Programme: Faculty building of 23,500
sq.m for 5000 students and 400
employees with four college halls,
12 small college halls, offices,
restaurant and meeting areas
with internet facilities
Design: 1991–92
Execution: 1993–95

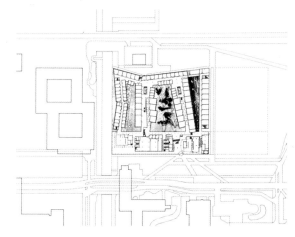

Site plan

Water patio

Front onto the canal

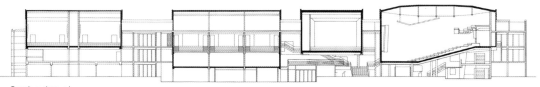

Section through
the auditoria

Zen patio

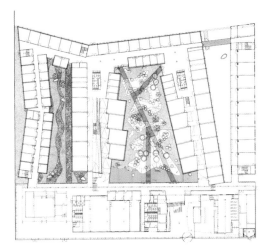

Ground floor

Interior galleries and ramps

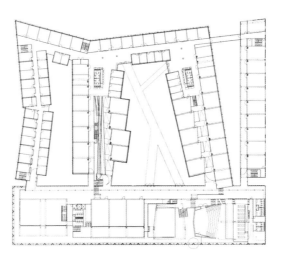

First floor

Toneelschuur Theatre
Haarlem (Netherlands)

Programme: Theatre in the historic
centre of Haarlem with two theatre
halls, two cinemas, a foyer, offices
and a loading bay, with a total floor
area of 5,400 sq.m. Designed
in collaboration with Joos Swarte
Design: 1998–2000
Execution: 2001–03

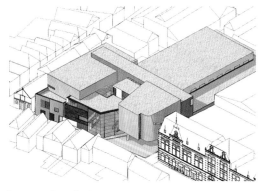

Axonometric projection
with insertion
into the context

Transparency between
the lobby and the street

View of the complex
from the street

Cross-sections

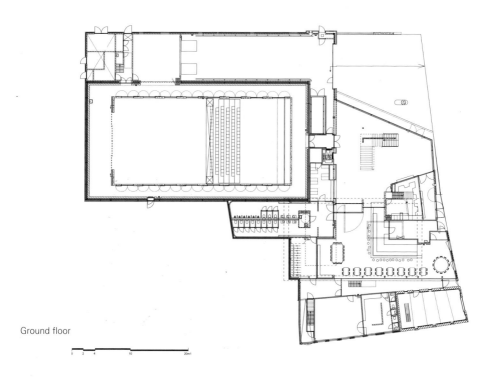

Ground floor

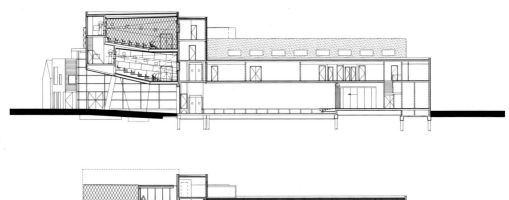

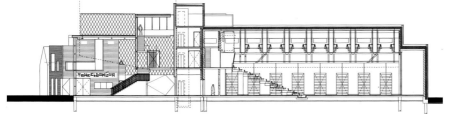

Longitudinal sections

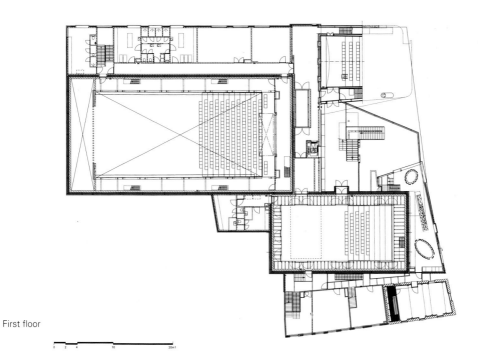

First floor

0 2 4   10   20m1

Interior of the lobby

Interior of the main theatre

MOdAM
Milan (Italy)

Programme: Multifunctional building
of 11,125 sq.m with a fashion school
of 3,910 sq.m, a fashion museum
of 5,215 sq.m and an underground
archive of 2,000 sq.m.
Design: 2006

Site plan

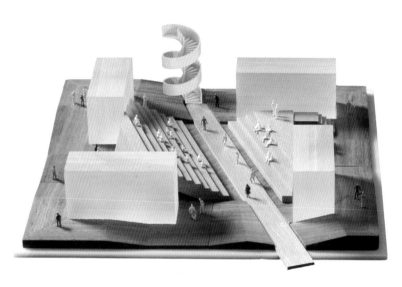

Working scheme
of the fourth floor

Fourth floor, spring exhibition

View of the insertion in the park

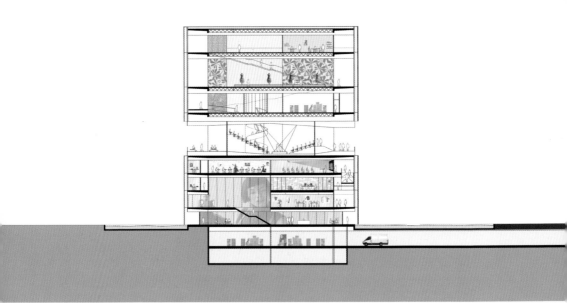

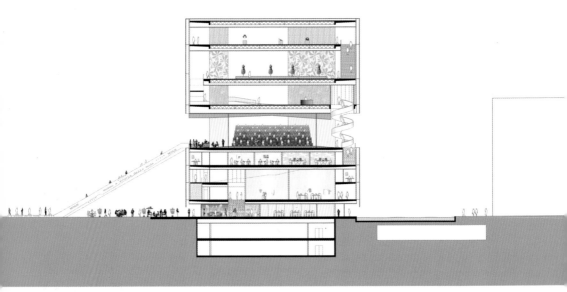

Sections

View of the internal
staircase

Materiality and Tectonics

When talking about the 'material delight' that characterizes the work of Mecanoo, we referred to the ambivalence between the role of expression and that of 'facing' of the construction, as well as to the dialectical relationship that emerges between materiality and spaces. This initial premise has to be developed by distinguishing between the tectonic role, i.e. that of revealing the structure, and the material role, i.e. the use of the 'physicality' of the building as a value in itself, independent of its load-bearing function. In fact, this distinction plays an important part in Mecanoo's work, offering a further means of expression that is integrated with the spatial and functional articulation.

In their tectonic choices, Mecanoo Architecten do not adopt a position favouring expression of the structural system (in line with Kenneth Frampton's interpretation of the Modern in *Studies in Tectonic Culture*), nor do they use the facing as a 'skin' to cover the structure (Semper's position). Nor do they necessarily go along with the most recent research into 'ambiguous envelopes' that reinterprets the notion of 'transparency' in an interactive key (as in the *Light Construction* exhibition organized by Terence Riley). All three of these lines of research are possible options and Mecanoo often employs different structural modalities within the same building in order to present it as a complex entity. The transitions between one structural system and the other become open spatial joints that support the idea of the 'crossing' of significant thresholds between parts of the programme and help in spatial orientation.

The materials play an alternative role to the tectonic divisions. They often divide a single shell into parts with different finishes that form 'themed' places: in doing this, they accentuate their role of 'artificial' facing and the notion of 'catalogue of options' set one alongside the other. In other cases, instead, a single element of construction is emphasized, accentuating its consistence (for instance the walls of recycled bricks laid with different types of course that are present in many works). In a third kind of use, the materials are 'layered' one on top of the other in an incomplete manner (as at Rochussenstraat) so as to gradually reveal a complex 'archaeology' of the building. The possibility of combining these different options shows that the positions adopted are not interpreted in a rigid way by Mecanoo (expression versus facing, legibility versus ambiguity) but as parallel opportunities for describing the complexity of the programmes, the institutions and the locations. In the immense mine of the Modern and the contemporary, the members of Mecanoo have discovered structural solutions to be re-examined, to be interpreted and modified, carrying out a 'transformation' that for them is more important than in-

'De Citadel' / Alexanderkazerne, The Hague (Netherlands). View of the brick shell

dependent invention because it reflects a rich cultural background. The origin of this indifference to building style is attributed by Houben to the encounter with Alvaro Siza during their collaboration on the design of the small house of the guardian of the car park in the housing complex completed by the latter in The Hague at the end of the eighties. That structure combined an abstract orthogonal frame with expressive volumes and enveloping brick surfaces, uniting the abstraction of the Nieuwe Bouwen with the expressionism of the Amsterdam School[1] in a paradoxical synthesis. Starting out from this example, Mecanoo embarked on a series of 'adventures' in construction.

The entrance pavilion of the National Heritage Museum in Arnhem is set like a screen between the forest and a lawn on which the various themed buildings of the exhibition stand. A large brick wall with a pattern of different finishes (almost a catalogue of traditional bricklaying techniques) is anticipated by a mysterious 'boulder,' a hemispherical structure clad in copper. Once past the wall/threshold, the pavilion unfolds into a brightly lit interior with glass walls and covered by a projecting horizontal roof. The floor is laid out on different levels and gradually leads visitors down into the ground, from where they can reach the egg-shaped shell of the boulder through an underground passage: it houses a cinema with a 360-degree screen visible from a rotating platform. Profoundly linked to the site, the pavilion opposes wall and open gallery, suspended and subterranean elements and real and simulated landscape with an eloquent alternation of different structural forms. But each of the components has a dual nature: the wall of bricks is apparently monolithic, but it is also fragmented by the different patterns of the bricks. The seemingly structural light pavilion is in reality clad with the wood of the frames and the ceiling; the 'boulder' seems rooted in the ground but is actually a lightweight metal frame. Thus the names assigned to them in the initial description of the project offer a partial view of reality that is then contradicted by a second reading.

The Isala College at Silvolde is a secondary school located by a river in the countryside in the western part of the Netherlands. A linear block with classrooms at the sides and a central road/corridor intersects a curvilinear volume containing the entrance hall, gym and library, forming a Y-shaped plan. The levels of the public part are staggered with respect to those of the classrooms and the steps at the entrance are transformed into a tiered arena that makes it possible to see all the levels of the building in section (the idea of the stepped hall and the staggered classrooms had been developed by Herman Hertzberger for the Apollo and Montessori schools in Amsterdam at the beginning of the eighties, but here the idea is given a more interactive treatment). The material used for the walls of the internal road and the classrooms is raw concrete while the ceiling is made of wooden boards. The exteriors of the linear block, screened by a metal colonnade, are faced with plywood panels on the front facing the river and brick walls at the rear. The two envelopes of the communal spaces are embedded one inside the other: the hall is clad in zinc and the gyms and library in burnished copper. The use of materials singles out the corridor as the core of the construction while the exteriors are screened and their facings 'break open' under the impact of the various blocks. The orientation of the wooden ceiling accentuates the horizontal trend of the internal road and reflects the light that filters through the walls of translucent glass from the outside.

Materiality as enveloping protection and the contrast between the interior and exterior of an enclosure are the themes that characterize the Emergis Centre for Psychiatric Health Care at Goes, in the Zeeland countryside. The complex is made up of two buildings with inner courtyards, a centre for the long-term residential care of forty-two psychiatric patients and a centre for geriatric psychiatry with twenty-eight patients. Both are based on the monastic typology of the cloister with a garden inside it. The exterior of the centre for long-term residential care is faced with planks of black-tinted pine and has just a few windows framed in white wood like those of the traditional farmhouses of the region, showing a clearly introspective orientation. The inner courtyard has a slender wooden colonnade that forms a portico at ground level and a gallery above, while the fronts of the rooms served by it are tinted in many different colours to distinguish the various spaces facing onto the courtyard. One corner of the enclosure is open and permits a view of the countryside outside from the courtyard, linking interior and exterior in a precise orientation. In the geriatric centre, on the other hand, closure of the courtyard was specifically ruled out by a requirement of the treatment programme that the elderly patients should not be isolated from the world outside. The communal rooms open onto the countryside through large glazed cuts that break down the black perimeter at precise points linked to the internal routes, while the courtyard is again screened with a colonnade. As can be seen, the contrasts between materials (dark and bright, tinted and natural) and between tectonic modalities (opaque facing and frame structures) delineate a precise spatial orientation that is closed to the outside while the inside opens onto spaces of greater privacy.

The relationship between a courtyard block and the open landscape organized through the materiality of the building is also the theme of the Hotel 'De Citadel' / Alexanderkazerne in the environs of The Hague, a residential complex of 444 rooms providing accommodation for officers of the Dutch Army and Navy. A linear block with a central corridor bends into four wings to form a trapezoidal courtyard that offers a view of a stretch of the surrounding landscape of sand dunes. The building is faced with orange-coloured bricks (as in the traditional architecture of The Hague), punctuated by horizontal courses of white stone that frame the sequences of strip windows of the rooms. The corners of the courtyard are treated as points of breakage in the envelope of walls: in fact most of them are glazed and contain the common staircases, offering precise views of the surroundings and therefore becoming significant public places that mark the entrances. The horizontal lines of the outer shell contrast with the tall dunes that have been left untouched, even in the vicinity of the building which appears to sink into the sand. A system of light metal walkways connects different points of the upper floors of the complex with the dune in the middle of the courtyard in a similar fashion to the Jungle Patio of the Faculty of Economics and Management in Utrecht. The contrast between building and ground, and their relationship through the perspectives of the internal road and the elevated walkways, results in a multiplicity of routes with urban as well as scenic characteristics.

Two recent projects, both for law courts, propose the contrast of inside and outside in two buildings treated as cities within the city. Both have a solid envelope cut by internal routes. The new Palace of Justice at Cordoba in Spain is a sort of casbah with narrow alleys that slice their way through a solid block, dividing it into nine volumes. Each of these also faces onto an inner patio: the routes erode the block in section too, creating stretches of covered road while the inner surfaces are faced with a geometric pattern of clearly Islamic inspiration. In the competition project for the extension to the courthouse in Trent, Italy, the existing courthouse is left as it is and its inner courtyard oriented toward a square that penetrates the new building with a flight of steps. This is formed out of a series of wings overhanging an alternation of public routes and patios that recall both the Faculty of Economics and Management in Utrecht and examples like Candilis, Josics and Woods' Freie Universität in Berlin. The front onto the square overhangs the public square on one side, a solution that was also employed in the La Llotja conference centre at Lérida.

Enveloping and suspended surfaces characterize the funerary chapel of Sankt Maria der Engelen in the Catholic cemetery of Rotterdam. Built on the site of a nineteenth-century church that had collapsed, the chapel presents the appearance of a light tent suspended over the ruins, touching the ground with nothing but slender pillars. The vertical curtaining consists of an encircling curved screen faced with zinc on the outside and painted blue on the inside. The roofing is another, lightly folded 'sheet' that forms a gold-painted ceiling. The joints between ground and envelope and between the latter and the roof are glazed, allowing light to enter at an angle and accentuating the reflective surface of the materials. Less tectonically determined than Mecanoo's other works, the chapel nevertheless offers an alternative to many works of funerary architecture, emphasizing the role of suspension and transitoriness: the hall inside is in fact a passageway with an entrance at each end and describes the ritual as a crossing.

The relationship between materials, tactility and spatial orientation is taken to an extreme at Visio, a school for visually-impaired children located at Huizen. To study the way the building would be experienced by its users, the studio's designers simulated the condition of partial blindness by wearing special dark glasses. They set out to create a building with 'tactile' but visually normal transitions so as not to isolate the patients in an atmosphere of 'exceptionality.' From this goal of integration emerged a two-storey complex with an H-shaped plan where the central wing is formed by a glazed atrium that offers a view of the surrounding landscape. The transitions between all the internal spaces are marked by a contrast between hard and soft materials or between surfaces that absorb sound and others that reflect it, distinctions that serve to guide the visually impaired. The classrooms have walls painted in bright colours that help partially sighted children find their bearings. The outer shell is also characterized by the contrast between the main block in pale brick and the volumes of the classrooms faced with planks of larch that are suspended above the main base.

The role of the curtain-wall as an ambiguous container somewhere between mask, window and layered wall is explored in the projects for the European Investment Bank at Luxembourg and for the seat of the World Health Organization in Geneva, both surrounded by green areas. While in Luxembourg the building is a sort of Möbius strip that sinks into and emerges from the ground by turns, in Geneva it is broken up into several pavilions that are scattered around the park and connected by narrow passageways. In Luxembourg the floors of the building come to a stop before the curtain-wall, while in Geneva there is a double-glazed and ventilated façade that presents a series of different corners towards the park. In both cases the idea of a themed landscape is developed through the relationship between the curtain-wall and the outside. However, this takes place in a different way in each of the two projects. In Luxembourg the interruption of the floor slabs forms an unbroken opening on the outside and, at the same time, presents a view of the building as if it were in section. In Geneva the double reflections of the two shells intersect the trees of the park in a continually shifting manner, bringing them inside or, alternatively, pushing them into the distance. In both cases an intermediate zone is created between the inside and outside that results in a visual interaction based entirely on perception in movement. There is no doubt that the interest in the landscape, at Arnhem as well as in these two projects, has been accentuated.

[1] Francine Houben/Mecanoo Architecten, *Compositie Contrast Complexiteit*, NAi Publishers, Rotterdam 2001. Published in English as: *Composition Contrast Complexity*, Birkhäuser, Basel-Boston-Berlin 2001, p. 7.

National Heritage Museum
Arnhem (Netherlands)

Programme: Entrance building
with museum and 'HollandRama'
panoramic theatre of 3,185 sq.m
Design: 1995–98
Execution: 1999–2000

Front onto the park

Entrance front with the brick
wall and the 'boulder'

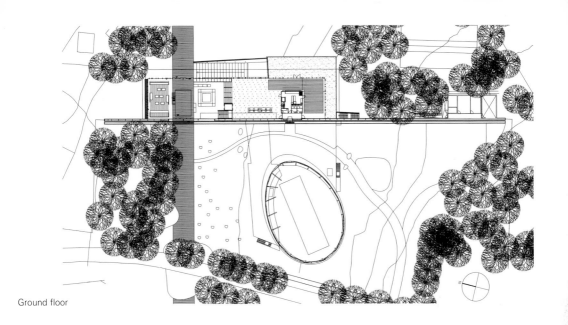

Ground floor

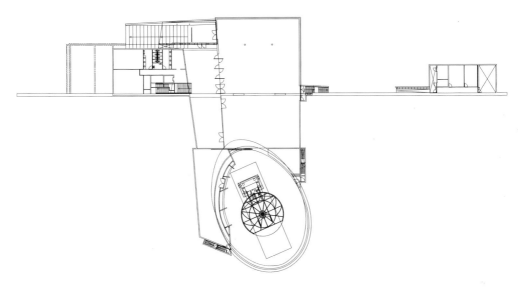

Basement

Glazed corner facing
onto the park

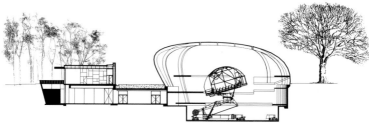

Section through
the underground auditorium

Interior with prospect
onto the park

Section

Isala College
Silvolde (Netherlands)

Programme: Secondary school
of 6,500 sq.m and extension
of 1.300 sq.m in the 'Paasberg' nature
reserve
Design: 1990–93
Execution: 1993–95

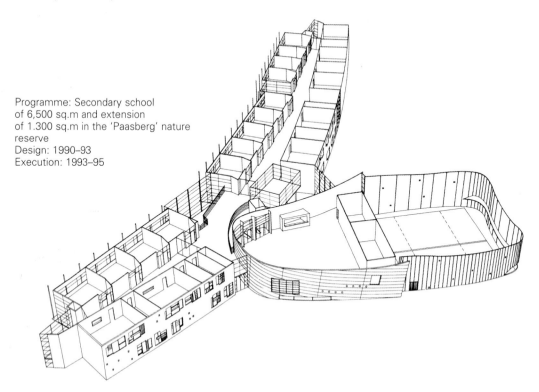

Axonometric cutaway

Front onto the row of trees

View of the arrival
at the building

The front with the gym

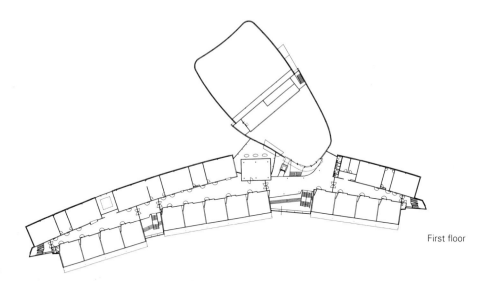

First floor

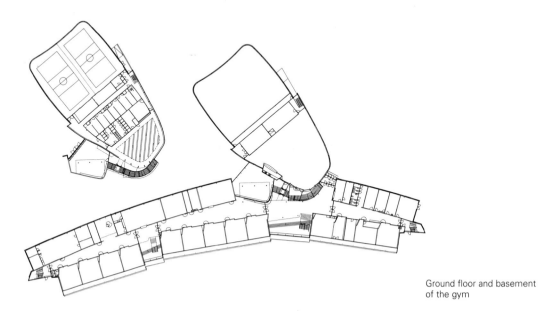

Ground floor and basement
of the gym

Internal plaza with multiple
levels opening on the
stair hall

Emergis, Centre for Psychiatric Health Care

Goes (Netherlands)

Programme: Pavilion for Long-Term
Residential Care of 1,800 sq.m
for long-term treatment of forty-two
psychiatric patients, Centre
for Geriatric Psychiatry of 1,740 sq.m
for twenty-eight patients
and 1,100 sq.m
of renovation
Design: 1995–2001
Execution: 2000–02

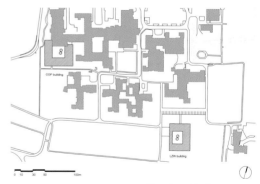

Site plan with the two
buildings

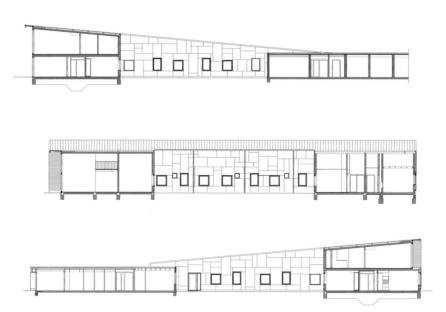

Geriatric psychiatry centre,
sections

Long-term treatment
centre, exterior shell faced
with wood

Long-term treatment
centre, courtyard

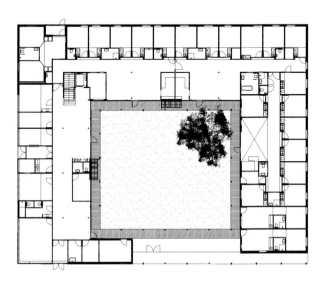

Long-term treatment
centre, ground floor

The courtyard from
the inside

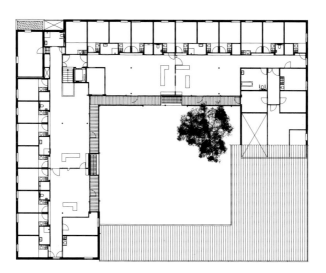

Long-term treatment
centre, first floor

'De Citadel' / Alexanderkazerne
The Hague (Netherlands)

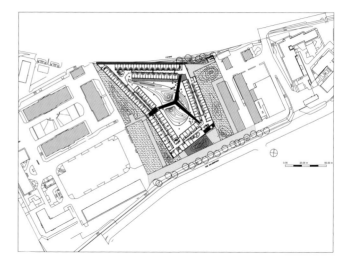

Site plan

Programme: Officers' hotel
of 16,435 sq.m with 444 rooms
for the Royal Dutch Army and Navy
Design: 2001–02
Execution: 2002–04

General view

Glazed north-east corner
of the courtyard

Internal road-corridor

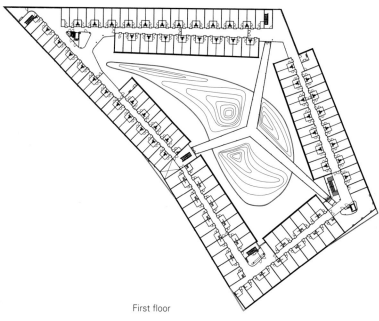

First floor

Entrance from the
courtyard on two levels

Courthouse
Cordoba (Spain)

Programme: Courthouse with
20 courtrooms, a wedding room,
a forensic institute, offices, a café,
an archive, prison and a parking
garage, for a total area of 48,000
sq.m. Design: Mecanoo with Ayesa
Competition Project: 2006, first place
Execution: 2008–11

View from the square

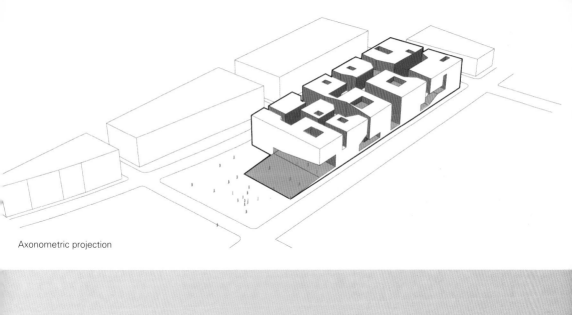

Axonometric projection

Second floor

Ground floor

Perspective longitudinal
section

View of an internal patio

Extension of the Courthouse
Trent (Italy)

Programme: Courthouse of 36,500 sq.m, of which 20,700 sq.m in new structures and 6,000 sq.m of renovation, 800 sq.m of public spaces and 9,000 parking places.
Design: Mecanoo in collaboration with Autonome Forme, Palermo
Competition Project: 2006, second place

Site plan inserted in the existing city

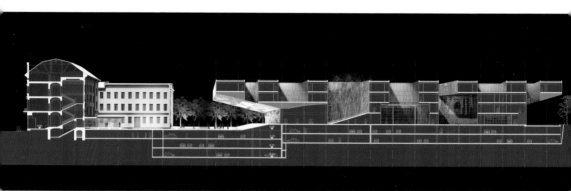

General cross-section

View from Via Pilati

View from the square

Public atrium

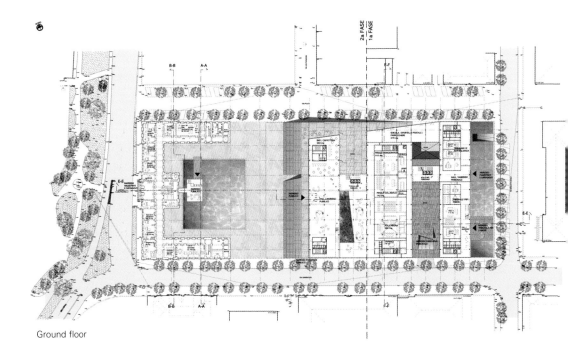

Ground floor

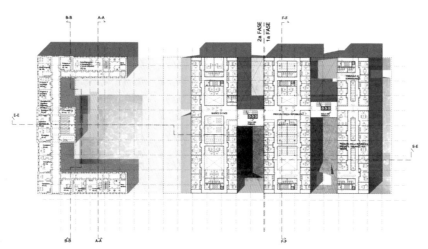

Second floor

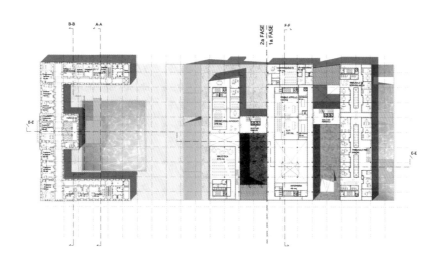

First floor

Catholic Chapel of Sankt Maria der Engelen
Rotterdam (Netherlands)

Programme: Catholic funerary chapel
of 120 sq.m built over the remains
of a nineteenth-century chapel
and design of the public space
Design: 1998–99
Execution: 2000–01

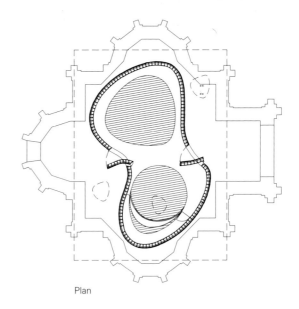

Plan

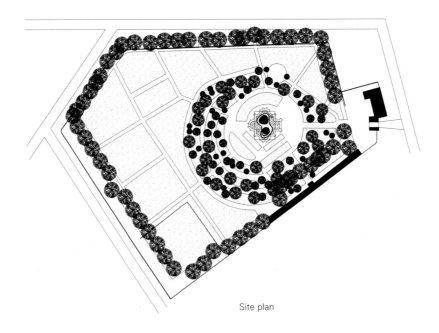

Site plan

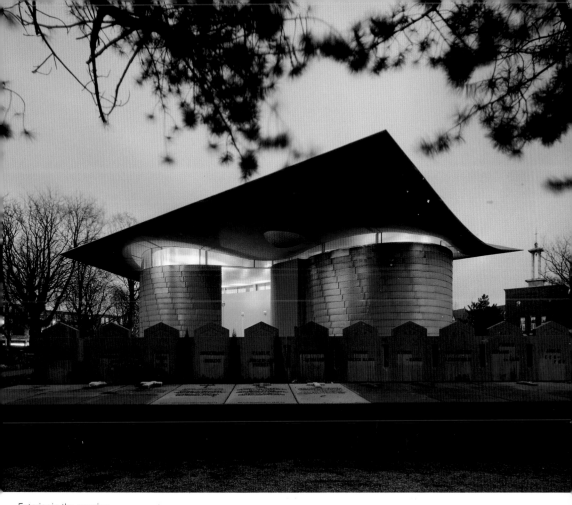

Exterior in the evening

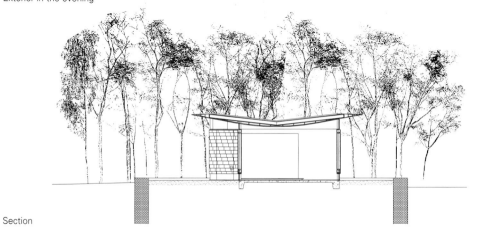

Section

Internal view of the blue
wall from the altar

Internal view looking
towards the altar

Visio, School for the Blind and Partially Sighted
Huizen (Netherlands)

Programme: School of 3,015 sq.m
for children with visual impairments
and multiple handicaps with
a gymnasium and therapeutic bath
Design: 2001–02
Execution: 2002–04

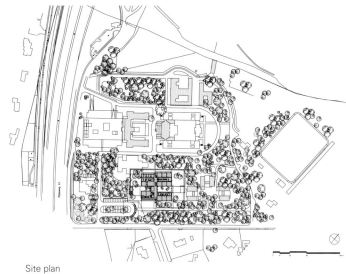

Site plan

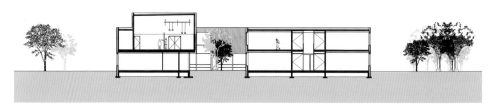

Cross-section

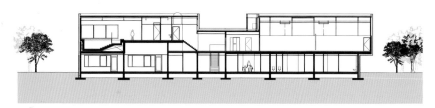

Longitudinal section

The glazed block between
the two wings

Interior

Ground floor

European Investment Bank
Luxembourg (Luxembourg)

Programme: Competition for the new
headquarters of 66,000 sq.m
Competition Project: 2002,
second place

General view of insertion
in the context

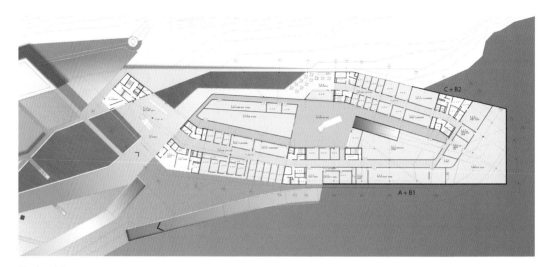

Plan level 0

Internal patio

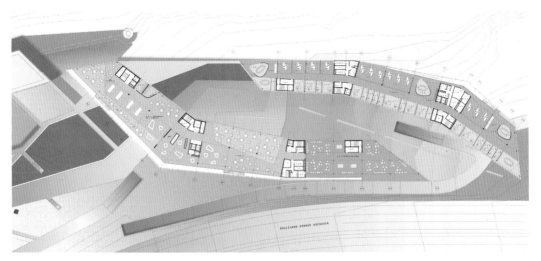

Plan level +6

View of the entrance front

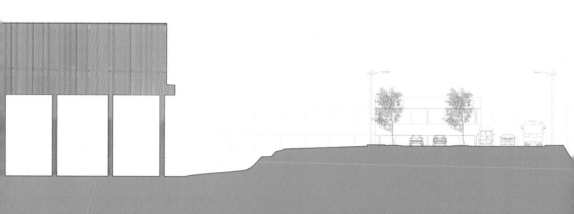

Cross-section

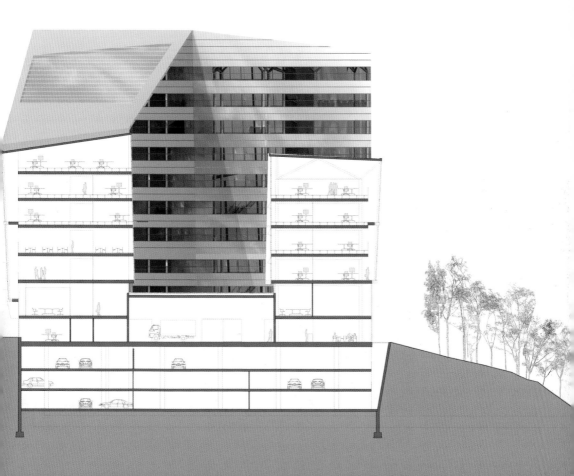

World Health Organisation
UNAIDS Headquarters
Geneva (Switzerland)

Programme: Competition for the
new WHO-UNAIDS headquarters
of 30,000 sq.m
Competition Project: 2002, first place

General aerial view

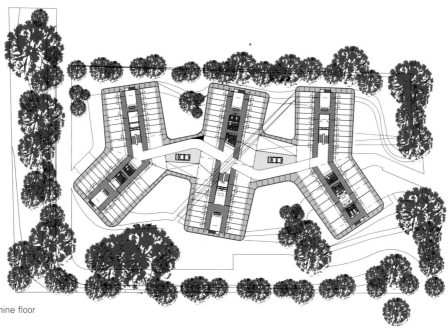

Mezzanine floor

View of the glazed wings

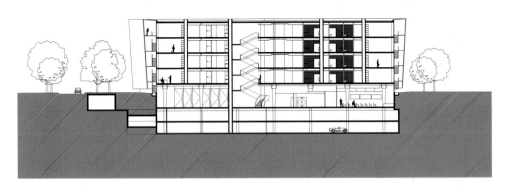

Section through the office block

Landscape-Buildings and Buildings in the Landscape

The Dutch landscape, lacking any high ground and to a great extent created by the reclamation of polders, often assumes the characteristics of a flat surface that can be artificially manipulated. Yet its real nature is dominated by a complex web of hydraulic balances, widely distributed among a myriad canals and subdivisions of farmland. The urban growth of recent decades has often led planners to treat the territory like a chequerboard, alternating new settlements and natural areas. As a result of this effort the landscape, radically modified, has taken on the characteristics of a composition, equivalent to that of built-up areas, and is often treated as a piece in an abstract pattern, an approach that is facilitated by the Dutch fondness for diagrams.[1] In parallel, in architecture, the absence of heights and the inexorable flatness of the territory have stimulated some designers to place pieces of artificial landscape in elevated positions. Nothing conveys this condition better than the work by the conceptual artist Jan Dibbets entitled *Dutch Mountains / Sea Hills*, in which a sequence of photographs of the sea arranged in a line is used to create a virtual mountain on the horizon. In recent architecture, this obsession with elevations has been translated into a vertical layering of landscapes at different levels (the MVRDV's Dutch pavilion at the Hanover Expo) and the treatment of the floor slab as an artificial slope (Koolhaas's designs for the library on the Jussieu Campus in Paris, the Kunsthal in Rotterdam and the Educatorium in Utrecht).

Mecanoo Architecten, attentive to the relationship with what already exists, have sought to give 'depth' to this artificial landscape and make it inhabitable without reducing it to a superficial reproduction of nature: this concern has led them to perceive as arbitrary the creations of many contemporary architects and their excessive indifference to physicality. The Library of the Delft University of Technology creates an artificial slope in front of the Aula, the main lecture hall on the campus that was designed by Van den Broek and Bakema in the sixties.[2] Beneath this inclined roof-garden all the functions of the library are located in a large colonnaded space that rotates around a big central cone in which the individual reading rooms are located. The cone emerges from the slope and allows light to enter from above, creating a perceptual link between outside and inside. The focal point of the space filled with columns is a large suspended wall of books painted blue that acts as a backdrop to all the activities that go on inside. The large, slanting ceiling has suggested distributing the functions in section and leaving as broad an opening onto the campus as possible at the sides. The outer walls that fill the gap between the real and the suspended ground are in fact glazed and supplement the illumination from the central core of the cone. Thus the library projects the slope outwards (towards the lecture hall) and inwards (with the cone).

So the creation of a raised public park is not seen as a division of levels but as an integration of the landscape into the definition of the interior and of a public space around the perimeter of the building.

The extension of the nineteenth-century villa converted into offices on the Maliebaan in Utrecht uses the stratification of the landscape as a way to establish a relationship with the existing building. Instead of adding a new block to house the extension, Mecanoo chose to locate all the new spaces underground and have them open onto a sunken patio set in front of the existing building. The ground is treated as an artificial element, but also as a 'layer' capable of housing the programme. The new section that has been created opens up the historic house to a new panorama (just as the library did for the lecture hall) and roots it in a new impression in the ground, an earthwork that echoes precedents in Land Art and the work of Emilio Ambasz. Here too the manipulation of the ground does not serve simply to 'reproduce' the landscape with an artificial construction, but to modify a context with preexisting structures by 'thickening' its section with parts of the programme set underground. Buildings inside and outside the ground look at each other through the new relief created by the project. As a result, this becomes creation of landscape-buildings and in parallel location of buildings in the landscape, never separating the two operations.

However different from one another, the project for the Industrion at Kerkrade and the recent scheme for the Philips Business Innovation Centre at Nijmegen (now under construction) should be seen precisely from this perspective of a mutual dialogue between artificial terrain and buildings that emerge from it. In the first case, a museum of industry in a mining area, the scheme divides up the 'mineral' nature of the context into the various parts that make up the whole. A large artificial mound of tailings (clay debris) partially enfolds an open-plan building organized around a repetitive structural grid and clad in tiles of various colours (the 'artificial' product of the mining industry). The whole thing is surrounded by a stockade of trees and faces onto a triangular basin of water that fronts onto the valley of the nearby river. A cylindrical belvedere set in the middle of the basin is reached from the building by a raised walkway. The purist flavour of the composition is contradicted by the material nature of the components, which recall the elements of an open-cast mine (heap of tailings, basin, shed) and house different functions.

In Nijmegen, on the other hand, two tongues of ground covered with grass (similar in conformation to the library in Delft) contain the public parts of the programme (car parks, a covered plaza, a commercial centre, auditorium and theatres) and form the base for three towers that stand out from it (one of the towers, the tallest and with a bent shape, has recently been constructed and is called FiftyTwoDegrees). The glazed space between two 'artificial mounds' becomes a public square. Thus the landscape creates different levels inside as well as outside, allowing the public to enjoy the view from the top of the hills or walk in the valley between them. In this project, urban and green areas are integrated to form a well-organized public space. Mecanoo has overcome the dichotomy between natural and artificial and softens the urban impact of the towers through a base that is revealed and concealed by turns.

The relationship between spaces covered by a slope and architectural object emerging from it is also to be found in the innovative project for the Learning Centre on the campus of the Lausanne Polytechnic. As at the Philips Centre, the services are located under a hill cut in half by a square, which penetrates into it and reveals it in section through large glass walls. On the top of the hill is set a block whose envelope has the aerodynamic shape of a wing and whose glazed front makes it look like a gigantic eye gazing at the landscape. The distinctive feature of this shell is that it turns on its central cylindrical support at a speed of fifteen degrees an hour, following the course of the sun and always keeping the windows away from direct exposure to its rays. The wing contains four levels: a first *bel-étage* that offers views of the space inside from broad terraces, a second public level that looks outwards instead, a third level with teaching laboratories and a fourth with a panoramic restaurant. The rotating tower (there is one in the Netherlands at Rotterdam, with a restaurant overlooking the harbour) is combined here with a landscape that is treated not just as a view in the distance but also as a base/artificial ground that supports the suspended element. Rooting and levitation, immobility and kinetics, natural and artificial, vision and materiality are contrasted here to create a fascinating and innovative structure that exploits its orientation to save energy and symbolize a new relationship between nature and technology.

The project for La Llotja conference centre at Lérida in Spain does not camouflage the building under greenery as at Delft or Nijmegen, but presents itself as an artificial spur that houses a sheltered space under its stone-clad overhang. The dynamic volume contains several auditoria on the raised floors which emerge from the roof like a mountainous landscape enriched with pergolas and creepers. Partially inspired by Van den Broek and Bakema's Aula in Delft, the conference centre has an opaque shell that opens along a raised horizontal line and creates two artificial landscapes above and below, multiplying the space public (*paseo* on the Segre River and urban park) on several levels. Inside, a large walkway leads to the main auditorium faced with red velvet, the gold-coloured multifunctional hall and the blue club, three shells that float in the semi-darkness of the large container and receive light from the elevated lounge that opens onto the outside like a suspended loggia.

The creation of artificial landscapes is never disconnected from contextual considerations, and they are viewed as relational elements that coexist with other realities (pre-existing buildings) in a complex setting. The dialogue between programmatic breaks, material discontinuities and 'inserts' of landscape is again to be found in the relationship between old and new, tackled by Mecanoo with imagination and daring. The attention to the landscape, moreover, has been gradually extended from complexes of buildings to the territorial scale because it is here that the challenge of the 'artificial landscape' is met at the public level.

[1] On this subject see: Svetlana Alpers, *The Art of Describing, Dutch Painting in the Seventeenth Century*, Chicago University Press, Chicago 1983, pp. 11–45 and Hans Ibelings, *The Artificial Landscape, Contemporary Architecture, Urbanism and Landscape Architecture in the Netherlands*, NAi Publishers, Rotterdam 2002, pp. 38–63.

[2] Mecanoo Architecten, *Bibliotheek Technische Universiteit Delft*, 010 Publishers, Rotterdam 2000, pp. 15–41.

Library of the Delft University of Technology
Delft (Netherlands)

Programme: University library
of 15,000 sq.m with underground
store for books, reading rooms, offices
for the university publishing house,
a room for the archives and for
the consultation of rare books
and exhibition area, study rooms,
bookbinder's workshop and bookshop
Design: 1993–95
Execution: 1996–98

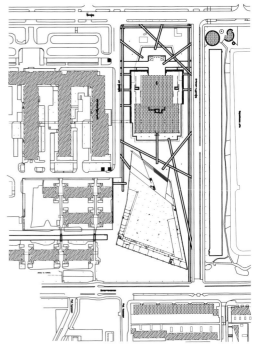

Site plan

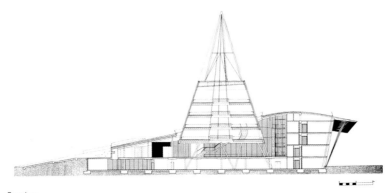

Section

The curtain-wall

General view

Ground floor, stacks

The wall of books

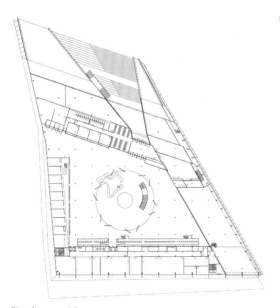
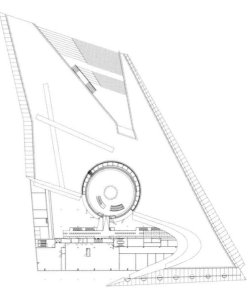

First floor – public entrance,
catalogues, newspaper
and periodical library

Upper level, reading rooms,
wall of books and offices

Interior with the cone

Office Villa Maliebaan
Utrecht (Netherlands)

Programme: Underground extension
and interior design of office-villa
of 980 sq.m
Design: 1996–97
Execution: 1998–2000

View of the sunken patio
from the offices

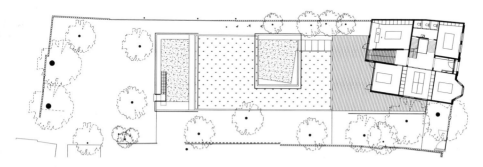

Ground floor
and longitudinal section

General view by night

Museum for Industry and Society
Industrion
Kerkrade (Netherlands)

Programme: New museum
for industry and craft in the mining
and industrial area of Kerkrade
Design: 1993

View of the model

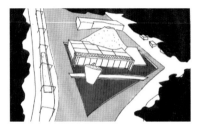

General view

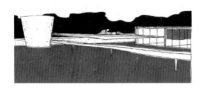

View from the river

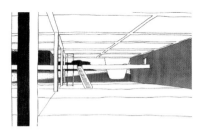

View inside the pergola lattice

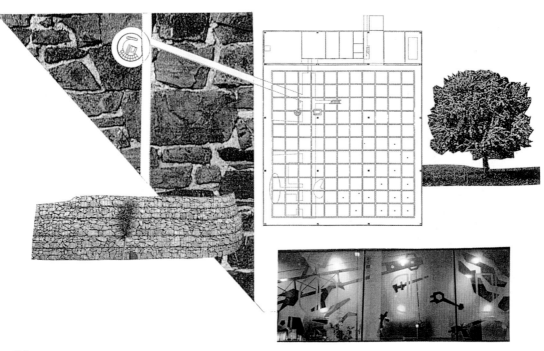

Collage

Philips Business Innovation Centre, FiftyTwoDegrees

Nijmegen (Netherlands)

Programme: Multifunctional complex
of 70,000 sq.m with offices,
a conference centre, catering,
apartments, retail and sport facilities
Competition Project: 2004–05,
first place
Execution: 2005–06

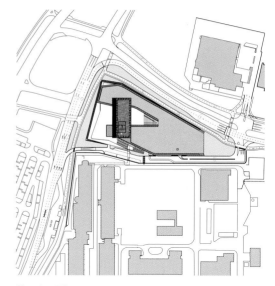

Site plan, FiftyTwoDegrees

FiftyTwoDegrees,
curtain-wall from the inside

FiftyTwoDegrees, front
and artificial mound

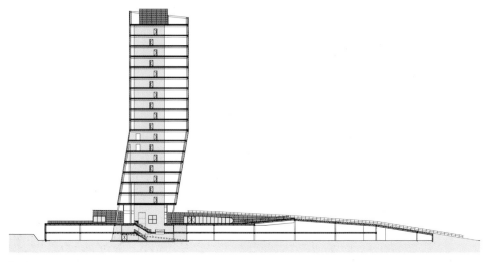

Section

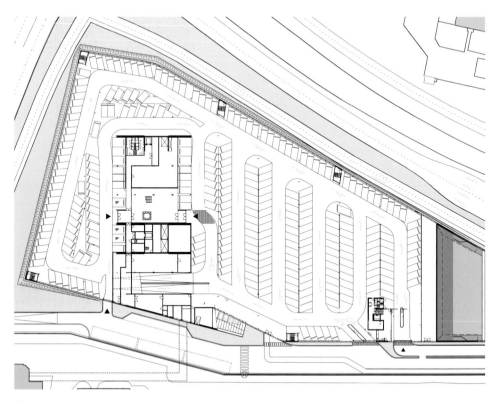

Ground level

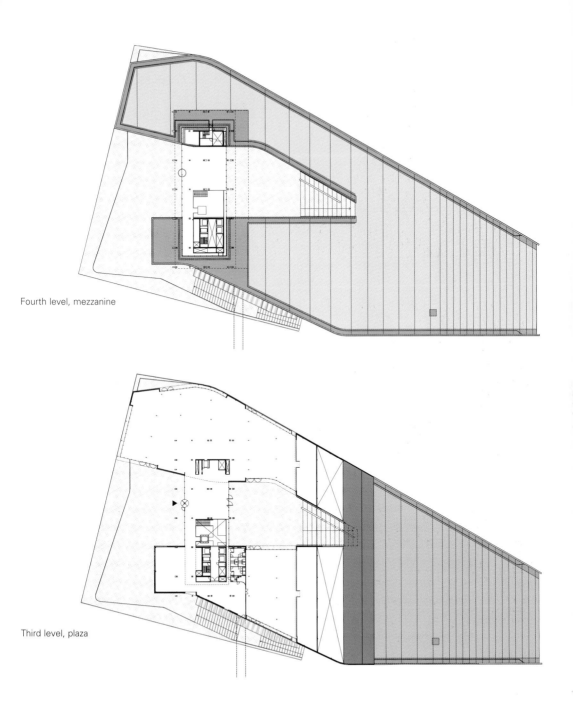

Fourth level, mezzanine

Third level, plaza

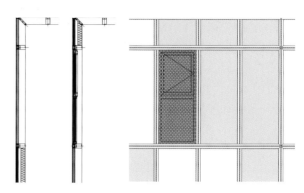

Detail of façade, front
and elevation

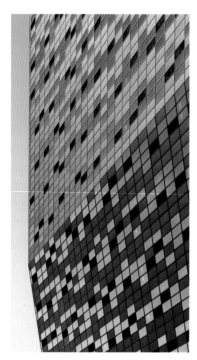

FiftyTwoDegrees, detail
of façade

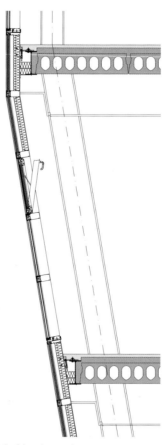

Detail of façade, section   FiftyTwoDegrees, profile

Learning Centre of the Ecole Polytechnique Fédérale de Lausanne
Lausanne (Switzerland)

Programme: Learning centre
of 15,000 sq.m
Competition Project: 2004,
second place

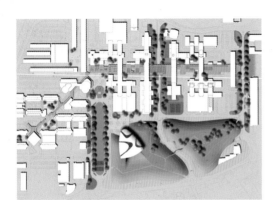

Site plan

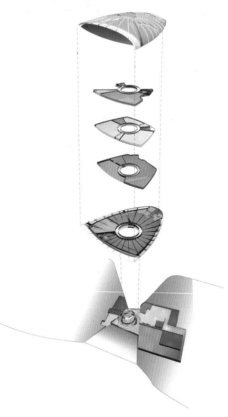

Axonometric exploded
drawing

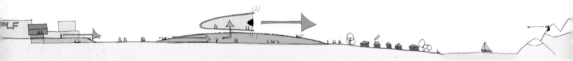

Concept, general section

View of the plaza, night
and day

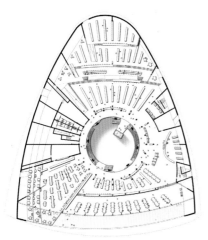

Level +1

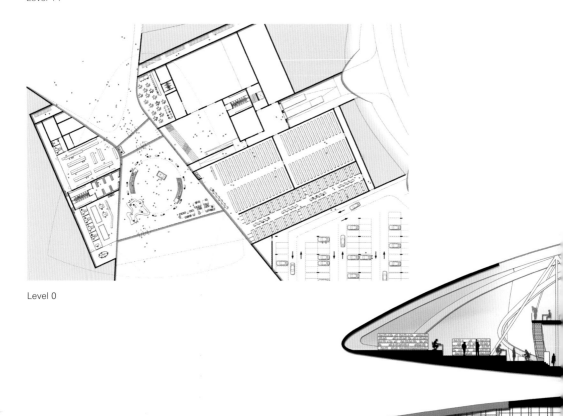

Level 0

Section

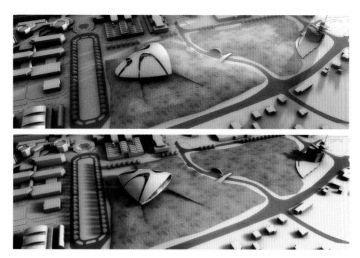

Rotation 1 and 2

La Llotja Theatre and Conference Centre

Lérida (Spain)

Programme: Theatre/conference centre of 37,500 sq.m with two conference halls (1,200 and 400 seats), the largest of which also functions as a theatre, a multifunctional space and lounge
Competition Project: 2004–05, first place
Execution: 2006–08

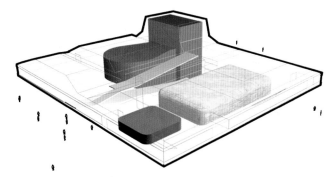

Axonometric scheme with the three auditoria: red, gold, blue

General view with insertion in the site

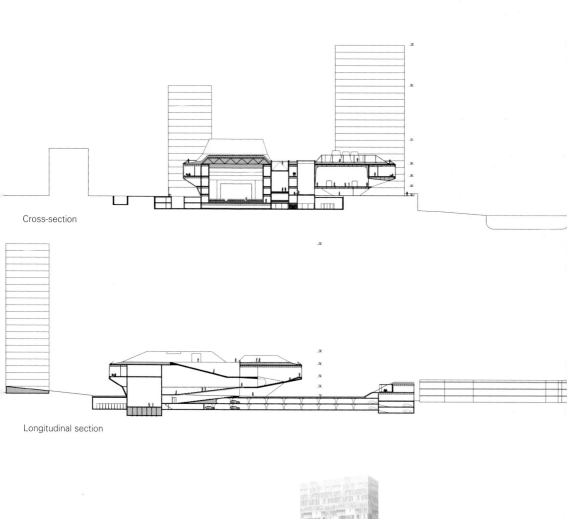

Cross-section

Longitudinal section

View from the road

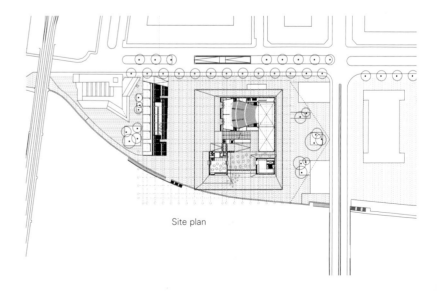

Site plan

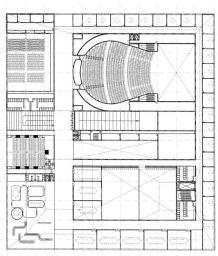

Level +2

Reuse and Conversion: Contrast as a Mark of Time

Some of the most significant examples of expressive representation of the functional programme through spatial gaps and tectonic-material differentiation can be found in the renovations and restorations of existing buildings carried out by Mecanoo. A number of principles of the studio's approach to history have been evident since 1994, with the project for the cultural centre in the ruins of Deurne Castle, and have been taken further in subsequent projects. One of these themes has been an appreciation of the time factor recorded in the materiality of the buildings. On the subject of Deurne, Francine Houben has written: 'Time goes on and must be respected as an autonomous being. The ruin of beauty is more beautiful than beauty itself'.[1] Tellingly, in that project the remains of the old castle were left as they were, the historic Dinghuis was violated by a contemporary block that emerges from it without any mediation and the new museum is an oblique metal volume with a copy of an old map of the place printed on its cladding. Mecanoo left the gaps between the buildings and worked instead on their context, connecting them with a deck and making them float in an expanse of water which reconstructs the former lake of the castle, which had disappeared after filling up with earth for centuries.

In this project, Mecanoo already saw the situation as one traversed by different incompatible durations, simultaneously present and not reducible to a single linear flow of time. The contemporary is placed alongside the old, creating a dialectical tension through the contrast between deliberately different languages. At the same time, the studio has proposed an ephemeral time that, in contrast with the slow accumulation of history, can be interrupted and removed. So the temporal hiatus is reversible and, as such, does not impose a reorientation on history but only a temporary modification of it. This is the principle that shapes Mecanoo's most interesting project of reutilization, the renovation of a neoclassical church in Amsterdam, built in 1793, for the experimental theatre group De Trust. The church had a large double-height nave with Tuscan columns supporting the galleries and over the course of time had been stripped of the organ in the apse and turned into a warehouse. Given the limited budget, Houben and her partners chose not to touch the façade and the floors inside, but simply to underline the patina of time with a grazing, theatrical illumination and to construct, in place of the organ, what they call a 'piece of furniture.' This is a light multi-storey structure independent of the walls and floors that houses various functions (bar, kitchens, stage machinery room) and contains the main staircase, from which the existing building can be glimpsed through openings as if it were an exterior. This plug-in structure, painted bright red to accentuate the contrast with the existing elements, can be removed or altered in the future without affecting the historic shell. Another piece of machinery is located in the hall, a self-supporting structure of tiered seating independent of the columns that can be removed, leaving the space free. A simple set of curtains forms the 'black box' of the theatre: in the daytime they can be opened and allow natural light to enter through the tall windows of the old church, turning the hall into a multipurpose room. The provocative contiguity of old and new, decayed and temporary and intervention and non-intervention creates a genuine installation that invades the space of the church.

The Rozentheater, one of Amsterdam's oldest cinemas (1912) and now disused, was also given a shock treatment in its conversion into a multifunctional youth centre through the materials and bright colours used to 'line' the foyer and auditorium. The bar is made of black recycled plastic and faces a red wall that alludes to the theme of roses ('Rozentheater' means 'Rose Theatre'). Fragments of films and texts are printed on the wall above the counter of the first floor of the foyer. The new glass balustrade that borders this mezzanine holds a dialogue with the stained glass windows of the historic façade, creating an interactive play of 'added' facings. In the 190-seat auditorium, the old tribune has been completely removed and there is now a flat floor and retractable seating that allow the space to be used both as a theatre and as a dance hall. Here too, the colour scheme is based on shades of pink, red and purple. New machinery and facings 'installed' in the existing shell declare their nature as temporary devices for performance, creating a triangular relationship between decoration, scenery and historic materials.

If in these two historic theatres it is the spectacle of the parts that Mecanoo Architecten have put on display, in the renovation of J.F. Staal's Stock Exchange in Rotterdam to create a foyer, council chamber and restaurant they took a more rigorous and unified approach. In fact they set out to re-create the Modernist-Deco atmosphere given the building by Staal but compromised by years of additions and alterations. White surfaces, streamlined corners and reflections from transparent and ground glass have restored the large hall illuminated from above to an abstract splendour that recalls the work of Staal without reconstructing it pedantically. It is interesting to note how, faced with a twentieth-century structure and a more institutional theme, Mecanoo came up with a modernist mimesis that re-creates an atmosphere which is more imaginary than real: that of the great vaulted atria and public buildings of the *reklamearkitektur* of the thirties. Modernism, a style which is much more fleeting than those of the past, is seen as an icon to be continually reaffirmed and not as 'hardware' to break away from. In this, Mecanoo Architecten have extended their notion of the ephemeral nature of the contemporary intervention (here handled in different ways) and their link with the Modern, reinterpreted here in the whole breadth of its problematic range.

[1] Francine Houben/Mecanoo Architecten, *Compositie Contrast Complexiteit*, NAi Publishers, Rotterdam 2001.

Pubblished in English as *Composition Contrast Complexity*, Birkhäuser, Basel-Boston-Berlin 2001, p. 115.

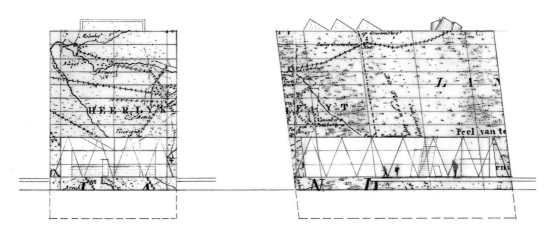

Deurne Castle (Belgium).
Profiles of the new
museum

Cultural Centre and Museum
Deurne (Belgium)

Programme: Restoration
and extension of a cultural centre
with museum, educational centre
and multifunctional spaces.
Design: 1994

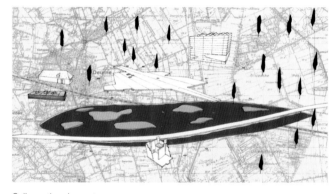

Collage, the elements
of the project

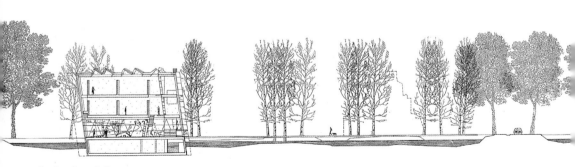

Section through the new
museum

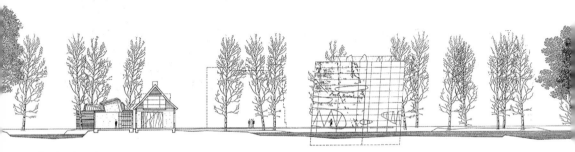

Section through
the Dinghuis

Ground floor of the island
with deck

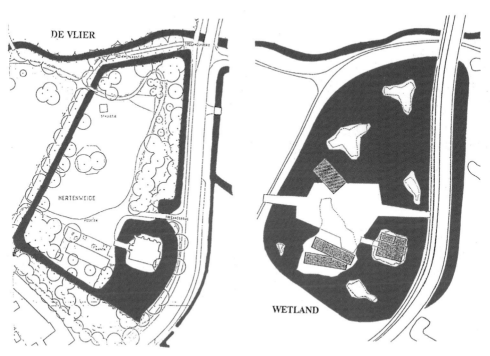

DE VLIER

HERTENWEIDE

WETLAND

Before and after reconstruction
of the marshes and the island

De Trust Theater

Amsterdam (Netherlands)

Programme: Conversion of a former
church into a theatre of 2,700 sq.m
Design: 1995
Execution: 1996

External view
of the neoclassical church

The theatre in the nave

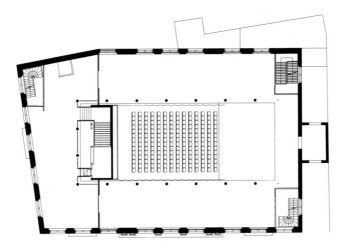

First floor

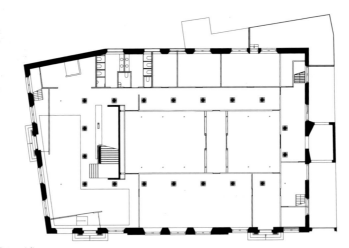

Ground floor

Entrance with, on the right,
the 'piece of forniture'

Rozentheater
Amsterdam (Netherlands)

Programme: Renovation of a theatre
to become a 2,100 sq.m youth centre
with a theatre hall (seating 190),
a multifunctional hall (seating fifty)
and a bar
Design: 2001–03
Execution: 2004–05

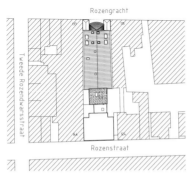

Site plan

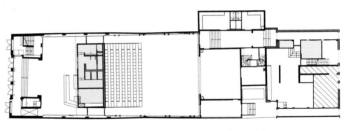

The façade

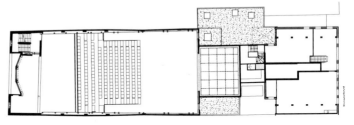

First floor

Ground floor

Interior of the new auditorium

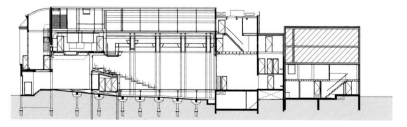

Section

Beurs – World Trade Center
Rotterdam (Netherlands)

Programme: Interior redesign
of 11,000 sq.m of the existing
building with a new entrance area,
new system of circulation, three
cafés/restaurants, offices, conference
rooms, shops, day-care nursery
and garage for parking
Design: 2002–03
Execution: 2003–06

Atrium from the entrance

Digital Port Rotterdam
installation

Atrium looking toward the entrance

Territory in Movement

Given the responsibility for planning entire districts, the members of Mecanoo developed a particular interest in problems on a large scale right from the beginning of their career. Very soon, however, the diversity of elements that characterized their housing complexes turned out to be necessary but not sufficient to tackle the dimension of the territory and the inclusion of the landscape in the creation of new towns, as happened all over the Netherlands after 1990. Mecanoo's sensitivity to the question of public interaction in buildings led the studio to develop planning strategies that set out to avoid both traditional zoning (with the assignment of different functions to different areas) and a 'design' of towns that aimed to enclose them in all-inclusive figures, as well as the new 'culture of diagrams' whose relationship with reality was perceived as schematic and distant. Thus they have pursued different directions of research:

1. A general attention to movement (in particular that of vehicles) as an element that binds together various events that occur on the territorial scale. This movement cannot be translated into planimetric figures, but only into sequences of views that record the unfolding of the perception of the territory in time, constituting a cinematic *storyboard* that unites the sequence shot (continuity) with cutting (the gaps). From this procedure it becomes clear that physical connection is of only relative importance to the recognizability of the territory and is overshadowed by the role of the 'intervals' and the empty spaces between more characterized places. This leads to the mutual definition of 'themed' urban zones and the design of the gap between them as a fundamental element of a 'rhythm' of settlement experienced in movement. This interest in intervals overcomes the distinction between urbanization and landscape and leads to both playing a part in the definition of a new territorial orientation designed for its users. The attention paid to the car never turns into a celebration of vehicular movement but is a recognition of its perceptual importance as a means of constructing 'continuity through discontinuity.'

2. Parallel to the concern with movement, there is an attention to the factor of time in the definition of space. We have already mentioned the strategy of 'drawing out' the definition of the plan into various intermediate phases so as to leave open the possibility of modification. This procedure is extended to the use of structures and settings: the members of Mecanoo consider various flows of time to be present simultaneously in their projects:

– an everyday time with the alternation of multiple uses of the same space by different people;

Aesthetics of mobility: analysis, the viaduct

– a time linked to nature and materiality in which the modification of the landscape, its seasonal cycles and the processes of aging of the buildings are considered factors that need to be planned for;

– a time of the gradual growth of settlements by stages, each of which assumes an identity (however temporary), and the possibility of 'controlled deviations' from the original forecasts of growth.

Mecanoo's penchant for complex phenomena of growth had already found expression in two projects in the mid-nineties, the planning of Almere up until the year 2015 and the redevelopment plan for the industrial area of the gasometers in Amsterdam. In the former the alternation between built-up area and patches of natural scenery was already present as an element of control over development in time; in the latter, the use of the existing structures as cultural containers was attuned to the series of the public events that were to be held in the complex (concerts, performances, utilization of the containers as theatre workshops, open-air festivals). Correspondingly, the presentation of both projects consisted of sketches, diagrams, views and sequences, without including an overall location plan.

The research into mobility undertaken by Francine Houben as consultant to the Ministry of Transport, Public Works and Water Management, culminating in her organization of the Rotterdam Biennial (under the title 'Mobility') in 2003, focused on perception in movement as a factor in territorial development.[1] Starting out from the assumption that mobility is an inevitable element in the expansion of settlement and in the daily lives of thousands of commuters (it is worth remembering that the Ranstad region, between Amsterdam, Rotterdam and The Hague, has the highest density of population in Europe and comprises several nearby cities served by high-speed trains and motorways), Houben formulated six categories of 'perceptual landscape' that could be used to describe the relations between urbanization and natural environment: the Panoramic Landscape (the traditional expanse of the Dutch countryside), the Eco-Viaduct (a tunnel that leaves the natural lie of the land intact), the Bali model (small-scale settlements surrounded by greenery), the Ruhr (orchestration of the alternation of green areas and industrial settlements), Las Vegas (urbanized sites characterized by commercial structures) and La Défense (high-density buildings constructed close to road infrastructures). In the model of territorial development perceived from the 'room with a view' of the car, Houben proposed the alternation of significant places (constructed typologies) and green spaces to create a 'rhythm' of orientation. This model of 'route' was contrasted with the notion of 'corridor' where sprawl creates an uninterrupted tunnel of undifferentiated settlements. The concept of route was then further developed to include other types of infrastructure (for example high-speed railways) and studied in conurbations in other parts of the world to find the differences between one context and another.

In the urbanized territory of the Ranstad, the intersections between infrastructures and built-up areas assume the role of nodes of aggregation and points of exchange between mobility and immobility. The analysis of mobility informs projects like that of the Van Hasselt Junction on the northern outskirts of Amsterdam, a meeting point between various flows: the rapid-transit railway, two motorways and a canal. Mecanoo took this complex interaction as a starting-point to propose a service and residential district that would form a true gate to the city, linking horizontal perception and intersection of movements. On a continuous base stand a series of tall blocks angled so that they can be perceived from various points in a dynamic way: in this way a layering of structures is formed that fosters both continuity and alternation.

The attention paid to the integration between car, built-up area and landscape has moulded other projects located in less strategic areas: the scheme for the Retailpark Westermaat at Hengelo, for instance, unites various shopping centres inside a green area enclosed by a fence of wooden slats, inserting them into a landscaped park and controlling the distances between supermarkets with a balanced distribution of the traffic. The same wooden slats are to be found around the innumerable towers that signal the presence of the complex at a distance: inspired by the historic vertical structures of the salt warehouses in the area, these light frameworks serve as a support for signs and combine the reference to tradition with an allusion to the agitprop structures of the Russian avant-garde of the twenties. Green enclosure and temporary landmarks, screening with landscape and signals of *reklamearkitektur* make Hengelo a thorough application of the theory of mobility that alternates architectural landmarks and affirmation of the value of the landscape as means of connecting up the new signs that line major traffic arteries.

The idea of a single enclosure and an internal common marked by a variety of individual elements was extended from Hengelo to a 'non-vehicular' place like the Hogeveld complex in The Hague, which is one of the blocks with a rectangular perimeter that make up a Vinex location. It includes two primary schools, a multifunctional centre, a sports hall, a day-care nursery and a block with six flats. Although the perimeter of the block is coherent, it opens up at various points, facilitating entry into a series of open spaces of a broken and varied shape. The fronts of the entrances to the various public functions are glazed (while the enclosure is a wall of brick) and clearly marked by illumination at night. They seem to carry the flow of traffic and ephemeral communication inside the block and look like open sections of a single building. They create a memorable public space where complexity, fragmentation and transparency interact, extending the notion of a vehicular route to urban pedestrian areas as well.

The intermediate and dynamic condition of the routes, as well as the organization of perception that they permit, make them an element that stitches together old and new settlements, the landscape and the built. Other 'pedestrian' projects carried out by the studio start out from this 'textile' approach to flows: as they proceed from one place to another, these flows branch out sideways into a series of ramifications, assuming a complex configuration. The figures of the zigzag route that 'stitches' various points together diagonally, the tree that projects its branches outwards, the amoeba and the rhizome have been developed by Mecanoo in projects like the Masterplan for the Campus of Delft University of Technology. The studio's partners took the covered paths designed by Oscar Niemeyer and Roberto Burle Marx for the Parque do Ibirapuera as the starting-point for this research, after visiting it on the occasion of their participation in the São Paulo Biennale in 1999.[2] The Brazilian architects linked the various exhibition buildings with a concrete roof whose plan echoes the shape of a tree with its branches. This horizontal plane creates routes but can also broaden out to form squares and enclose internal functions (it is also worth recalling here Raul Carlos Villanueva's system of covered routes for Caracas University, which perhaps plays an even stronger role as a binder for the various buildings than the roof at Ibirapuera). Mecanoo developed this idea at Delft, placing two 'servers' on the main axis of the campus, roofs with an undefined plan that connect the entrances of all the existing buildings as well as containing conference halls.[3] Niemeyer's 'dancing' roof encounters the diagram of multiple lateral routes branching off from a linear axis to form a multifunctional work of architecture open to unexpected developments.

[1] See: Francine Houben (ed.), *Mobility: A Room with a View*, NAi Publishers, Rotterdam 2003.

[2] Francine Houben/Mecanoo Architecten, *Compositie Contrast Complexiteit*, NAi Publishers, Rotterdam 2001.

Published in English as: *Composition Contrast Complexity*, Birkhäuser, Basel-Boston-Berlin 2001, pp. 211–12.

[3] Mecanoo Architecten, *TU Delft Masterplan*, Delft University Press 2002, pp. 19–30.

Masterplan for the Campus
of Delft University
of Technology, Delft
(Netherlands), design
2001–02. View of the public
pedestrian area

The Art of Engineering
and the Aesthetics of Mobility

Programme: Project on the motorway
as design resource from
the perspective of the road user
Design: 1999

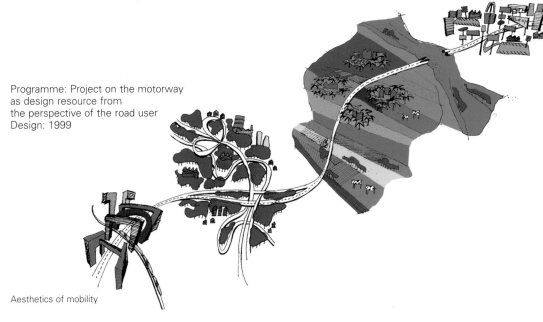

Aesthetics of mobility

Analysis, the motorway

Las Vegas

La Défense

Bali

Ruhr

Panoramic landscape

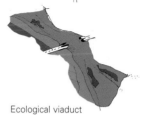

Ecological viaduct

Corridor

Route

Van Hasselt Junction
Amsterdam (Netherland)

Programme: Masterplan for
a multifunctional program that includes
approximately 58,000 sq.m
of apartments and offices at an
infrastructural junction between
the North-South Line, the IJ-Tunnel
Route and the main traffic link
to Amsterdam North
Design: 2001

View from the canal

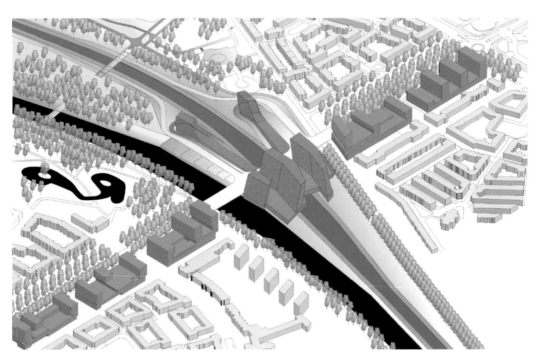

Axonometric projection
of insertion in the context

View from Adelaarsweg

View from the north

Retailpark Westermaat Shopping Centre
Hengelo (Netherlands)

Programme: Urban plan for a retail park with an Ikea of 25,000 sq.m, advertisement towers, commercial space of 25,000 sq.m and a McDonald's of 470 sq.m
Design: 1999–2002
Execution: 2001–04

Site plan, phase 3

View from the motorway

Night-time view
with advertising totem

Front by night

Front by day

Hogeweld
The Hague (Netherlands)

Programme: Multifunctional complex of 13,500 sq.m that includes two elementary schools, a multifunctional centre of 1,500 sq.m, a sports hall of 2,800 sq.m, a day-care centre of 1,400 sq.m and six apartments of 115 sq.m within the 'Hoge Weld' urban plan
Design: 2000–02
Execution: 2003–04

Plan of insertion in the Vinex estate

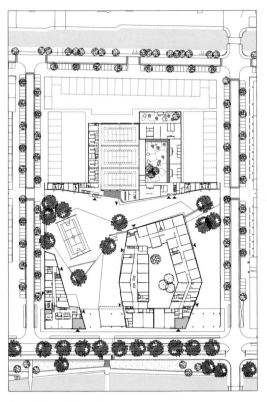

Ground floor of the entire complex

Overall view at night:
on the left the sports centre,
on the right the schools

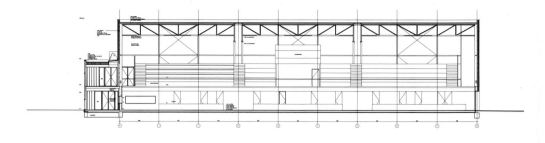

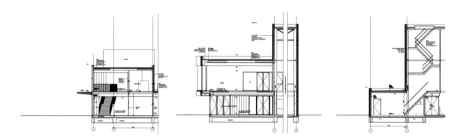

Sections of the sports
centre

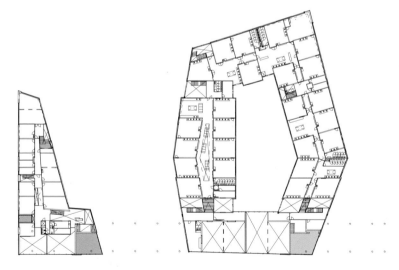

First floor of the schools

Relationship between
curtain-wall and buildings
on the first floor

Curtain wall of the entrance
to the sports centre
and patio

Patio next to the sports
centre

Interior

Masterplan for the Campus
of Delft University of Technology
Delft (Netherlands)

Programme: Masterplan
for the 60,000-sq.m campus
of the TU Delft. Mecanoo
in collaboration with TU Delft
Vastgoed and ING Real Estate, The
Hague
Design: 2001–02 for the masterplan,
2005 for Mekelpark

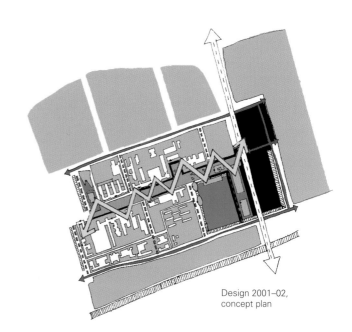

Design 2001–02,
concept plan

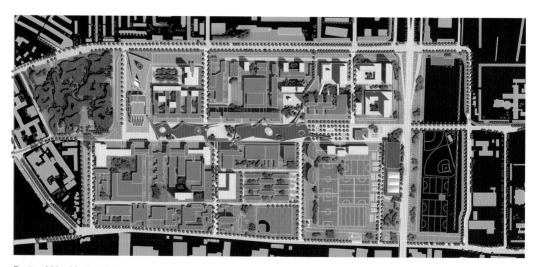

Design 2001–02, site plan

Design 2001–02,
view of the model

Design 2001–02,
concept view

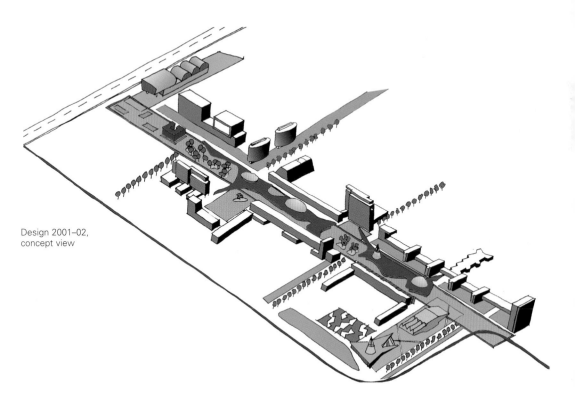

Design 2001–02,
view of the servers

List of Works

Innovators in Housing

Vondelpark
Vondellaan, Utrecht
(Netherlands)
Programme: urban planning
for 19,600 sq.m of public
space and design of 203
housing units
Design: 1998–99
Execution: 2000–02
Client: Proper-Stok
Woningen B.V., Rotterdam
i.s.m. Gemeente Utrecht;
Proper-Stok Woningen B.V.,
Rotterdam i.s.m.
Gemeente Utrecht
General Contractor:
Reinbouw b.v., Dieren
Structural Engineer:
ABT b.v., Delft
Plant Engineer: DGMR
Raadgevende Ingenieurs
b.v., Arnhem

Ringvaartplasbuurt Oost
Jacques Dutilhweg, Ariana
Noorlandensingel, Geertrui
Henningstraat, Neeltje
Griffijnstraat, Klaas
Dullemondstraat,
Geertruida Breurstraat,
Clazina Kouwenbergzoom
(Netherlands)
Programme: urban plan
for the residential
development of an area
of 10 hectares with 550
dwellings
Design: 1988–91
Execution: 1991–93
Client: Stichting
Volkswoningen, Rotterdam
General Contractor:
Volker Bouwmaatschappij,
Rotterdam
Structural Engineer:
Groenendijk en Poot,
Rotterdam

Herdenkingsplein
Herdenkingsplein,
Maastricht (Netherlands)
Programme: fifty-two

housing units and a square
in the historic centre
of Maastricht
Design: 1990–92
Execution: 1993–94
Client: Stichting
Pensioenfonds Rabobank,
Utrecht (residenze)
en Gemeente Maastricht
(piazza)
General Contractor:
Bouwmaatschappij Keulen
b.v., Geleen
Structural Engineer:
ABT b.v., Delft/Velp

Nieuw Terbregge
Willy Lagermanstraat,
Marie Baronstraat,
Zus Braunstraat,
Willy den Oudenstraat,
Piet van de Polsingel,
Rotterdam (Netherlands)
Programme: urban plan
for 107 'double-deckers'
and 48 waterfront houses
for a total floor area
of 24,655 sq.m
Design: 1998
Execution: 1999–2001
Client: Proper-Stok
Woningen B.V., Rotterdam
General Contractor:
Volker Bouwmaatschappij,
Rotterdam
Structural Engineer:
Adviesburo J.J. Datema
b.v., Woudenberg
Energy Efficiency
Consultant: W/E Adviseurs
Duurzaam Bouwen

Oeverpad
Oeverpad, Osdorp,
Amsterdam (Netherlands)
Programme: Residential
building with 120
apartments of sizes varying
from 104 to 168 sq.m
covering a total area of
20,000 sq.m and car park
Design: 2002–03
Execution: 2003–05
Client: Proper-Stok

Woningen B.V., Rotterdam
General Contractor:
Heijmans IBC Bouw,
Almere
Management consultant:
Mondiales Folies,
Rotterdam; Atelier
Bouwkunde, Rotterdam
Structural Engineer:
Grondmij van Ruitenburg,
Houten
Mechanical and Electrical
Engineer: Breman Noord-
Holland, Heerhugowaard;
Wolf + Dikken adviseurs,
Wateringen
Building Costs Consultant:
Basalt Bouwadvies b.v.,
Nieuwegein
Technical Engineer: Breman
Noord-Holland,
Heerhugowaard

Houben House and
Studio
Rotterdam (Netherlands)
Programme: House
with studio of 300 sq.m
Design: 1989–90
Execution: 1990–91
Client: Francine Houben
General Contractor:
Van Omme & de Groot b.v.,
Rotterdam
Structural Engineer:
ABT b.v., Delft/Velp
Technical Engineer:
Ketel Raadgevende
Ingenieurs b.v., Delft

Hybrid Buildings,
Coexistence of Functions

Rochussenstraat
Rochussenstraat,
Rotterdam (Netherlands)
Programme: Multifunctional
building of 12,000 sq.m
with offices, shops,
apartments and garage
for parking
Design: 1991–92
Execution: 1993–95

Client: Woningbedrijf
Rotterdam, Stichting
Sophia Logeerhuis Ouders
Rotterdam, Parkeerbedrijf
Rotterdam,
Gemeentepolitie
Rotterdam, Westpoint
Beheer Rotterdam
General Contractor: ERA
Bouw b.v., Zoetermeer
Structural Engineer:
Bouwkundig Adviesburo
Baas b.v., Rotterdam
Technical Engineer:
Technisch Adviesbureau
Jac. Nieuwenburg b.v.,
The Hague
Supervision: Bureau
voor Bouwkunde b.v.,
Rotterdam

**Oude Torenstraat
Complex**
Oude Torenstraat,
Hilversum (Netherlands)
Programme: 18
apartments, 2,700 sq.m
of offices and commercial
spaces and a garage for
parking in the city centre
Design: 1995–97
Execution: 1999–2000
Client: Johan Matser
Projectontwikkeling b.v.,
Hilversum
General Contractor:
BK Bouw, Bussum
Progettazione Strutturale:
Ingenieursgroep van
Rossum, Almere
Structural Engineer:
DGMR Raadgevende
Ingenieurs b.v., Arnhem
Consulting Engineers:
Valstar Simonis
Raadgevende Ingenieurs,
Rijswijk
Energy Efficiency
Consultant: GIZEH b.v.,
Amersfoort

Montevideo
Wilhelminapier,
Landverhuizersplein,

Rotterdam (Netherlands)
Programme: 153-m-high
tower with total floor area
of 57,530 sq.m, including
36,867 sq.m of apartments,
905 sq.m of pool, fitness
and service space, 6,129
sq.m of offices, 1,608 sq.m
of shops and a garage
of 8,413 sq.m for parking
Design: 1999–2003
Execution: 2003–05
Client: ING Real Estate,
The Hague
General Contractor:
Besix, Brussel
Structural Engineer:
ABT b.v., Delft
Mechanical and Electrical
Engineer: De Boer en Post
technisch adviesbureau
b.v, Heerhugowaard
Consulting Engineers:
Adviesbureau Peutz &
Associes b.v, Zoetermeer

Lange Jan and Lange Lies
Heerlen (Netherlands)
Programme: Pair of
residential towers, each
of 15,000 sq.m, with 31 and
25 floors respectively and
housing 110 apartments
Design: 2003–04
Client: 3W Vastgoed b.v.,
Heerlen; Vesteda Project
b.v., Maastricht; Gemeente
Heerlen
Structural Engineer: ABT
b.v., Delft

**'Canadaplein' Cultural
Centre and Theater
De Vest**
Canadaplein, Alkmaar
(Netherlands)
Programme: Cultural centre
of 9,300 sq.m with museum,
library and music school.
In the theatre: restoration
of the foyer, small theatre,
café and a 4.175 sq.m
educational centre
Design: 1998–1999

Execution: 1999–2000
Client: Gemeente Alkmaar
General Contractor:
Bouwbedrijf M.J. de Nijs
en Zn. b.v., Warmenhuizen
Management Consultant:
Temid Raadgevende
Ingenieurs b.v.,
Heerhugowaard
Structural Engineer:
Cumae Projectmanagers
en Ingenieurs b.v., Arnhem
Consulting Engineers:
Adviesbureau Peutz en
Associes b.v., The Hague
Mechanical and Electrical
Engineer: Valstar Simonis
raadgevende ingeneurs,
Rijswijk
Exhibition Design:
Platvorm, Amsterdam;
Studio 32, Amsterdam

**Laboratories
and Research Centre,
Novartis Campus**
Fabrikstrasse /
Hunigerstrasse, Basel
(Switzerland)
Programme: Innovative
laboratory and knowledge
centre of 10,000 sq.m
Design: 2003
Client: Novartis Pharmacie
AG, Basel
Structural Engineer:
Arup b.v., Amsterdam
Building Costs Consultant:
Basalt Bouwadvies b.v.,
Nieuwegein
Technical Engineer: Arup
b.v., Amsterdam; Arup,
London; Arup, Cork

**Faculty of Economics
and Management,
Utrecht University**
Padualaan 101, Utrecht
(Netherlands)
Programme: Faculty
building of 23,500 sq.m
for 5000 students and 400
employees with four
college halls, 12 small

college halls, offices,
restaurant and meeting
areas with internet facilities
Design: 1991–92
Execution: 1993–95
Client: Stichting
Financiering Exploitatie
Huisvesting Uithof, Utrecht
General Contractor:
Hollandsche Beton
Maatschappij b.v., Utrecht
Management Consultant:
PRC Management
Consultants b.v.,
Bodegraven
Structural Engineer:
ABT b.v., Delft/Velp
Mechanical and Electrical
Engineer: Technical
Management b.v.,
Amersfoort
Artists: Gera van der Leun,
Henk Metselaar, Linda
Verkaaik
Landscape: Van Ginkel b.v.,
Veenendaal

Toneelschuur Theatre
Lange Begijnestraat 9,
Haarlem (Netherlands)
Programme: Theatre
in the historic centre
of Haarlem with two
theatre halls, two cinemas,
a foyer, offices and
a loading bay, with a total
floor area of 5,400 sq.m.
Designed in collaboration
with Joos Swarte
Design: 1998–2000
Execution: 2001–03
Client: Gemeente Haarlem;
de Toneelschuur, Haarlem
General Contractor:
Bouwbedrijf M.J.
de Nijs en Zonen b.v.,
Warmenhuizen
Structural Engineer:
ABT b.v. Delft
Special Plant and Acoustic
Engineer: Dorsserblesgraaf,
The Hague
Building Costs Consultant:
Basalt bouwadvies b.v.,

Nieuwegein
Electrical Engineer: Halmos
b.v., The Hague
Mechanical and Electrical
Engineer: Halmos b.v.,
The Hague

MOdAM
Porta Nuova Gardens,
Milan (Italy)
Programme: Multifunctional
building of 11,125 sq.m
with a fashion school
of 3,910 sq.m, a fashion
museum of 5,215 sq.m
and an underground archive
of 2,000 sq.m.
Design: Mecanoo in
collaboration with Cerasi &
De Agostini Architetti and
Luca Molinari
Design: 2006
Client: Municipality of Milan
Structural Engineer:
ABT b.v., Delft;
Politecnica–Ingegneria
e Architettura, Milano
Mechanical and Electrical
Engineer:
Politecnica–Ingegneria
e Architettura, Milano

Materiality and Tectonics

National Heritage
Museum
Schelmseweg 89,
Arnhem (Netherlands)
Programme: Entrance
building with museum
and 'HollandRama'
panoramic theatre of 3,185
sq.m
Design: 1995–98
Execution: 1999–2000
Client:
Rijksgebouwendienst
Directie Oost; Nederlands
Openluchtmuseum,
Arnhem
General Contractor:
Strukton Bouwprojecten
b.v., Maarssen

Management Consultant:
ARBA MINCH
projectmanagement b.v.,
The Hague
Structural Engineer:
Goudstikker-de Vries / ACN
b.v., Capelle a/d IJssel
Technical Engineer:
Technical Management,
Amersfoort

Isala College
Laan v. Schuylenburg 8,
Silvolde (Netherlands)
Programme: Secondary
school of 6,500 sq.m and
extension of 1,300 sq.m
in the 'Paasberg' nature
reserve
Design: 1990–93
Execution: 1993–95
Client: Katholieke Stichting
voor Voortgezet Onderwijs,
regione Oude IJssel
General Contractor:
Klaassen
Bouwmaatschappij,
Dinxperlo
Structural Engineer:
ABT b.v., Delft
Mechanical and Electrical
Engineer: Ketel
Raadgevende Ingenieurs,
Delft

Emergis, Centre for
Psychiatric Health Care
Oostmolenweg 101,
Goes (Netherlands)
Programme: Pavilion
for Long-Term Residential
Care of 1,800 sq.m
for long-term treatment
of forty-two psychiatric
patients, Centre for
Geriatric Psychiatry of
1,740 sq.m for twenty-
eight patients and 1,100
sq.m of renovation
Design: 1995–2001
Execution: 2000–02
Client: Emergis, Centrum
voor Geestelijke
Gezondheidszorg, Goes

General Contractor:
Bouwgroep Peters b.v.,
Middelburg
Structural Engineer:
ABT b.v., Delft
Technical Engineer: Wolter
& Dros Groep, Goes
Energy Efficiency
Consultant: DGMR
Raadgevende Ingenieurs,
The Hague

'De Citadel' /
Alexanderkazerne
Oude Waalsdorperweg,
The Hague (Netherlands)
Programme: Officers' hotel
of 16,435 sq.m with 444
rooms for the Royal Dutch
Army and Navy
Design: 2001–02
Execution: 2002–04
Client: Heijmans IBC Bouw,
Capelle a/d IJssel
General Contractor:
Heijmans IBC Bouw,
Capelle a/d IJssel
Structural Engineer:
ABT b.v., Delft
Consulting Engineers:
DGMR b.v., The Hague;
Dorsserblesgraaf, Blesgraaf
Mechanical and Electrical
Engineer: Halmos
adviseurs, The Hague
Building Costs Consultant:
Basalt Bouwadvies,
Nieuwegein
Energy Efficiency
Consultant: Halmos
adviseurs, The Hague

Courthouse
Area between Calle Isla
Mallorca, Calle Isla
Formentera, Calle Isla
Gomera, Calle Cantabrico,
Cordoba (Spain)
Programme: Courthouse
with 20 courtrooms,
a wedding room, a forensic
institute, offices, a café,
an archive, prison and
a parking garage, for a total

area of 48,000 sq.m. Design:
Mecanoo with Ayesa
Competition Project:
2006, first place
Execution: 2008–11
Client: Consejería de
Justicia y Administración
Pública, Sevilla, Spain
/ Ayesa, Sevilla
Structural and Plant
Engineer: Ayesa, Sevilla

Extension of the
Courthouse
Via Pilati, Trent (Italy)
Programme: Courthouse
of 36,500 sq.m, of which
20,700 sq.m in new
structures and 6,000 sq.m
of renovation, 800 sq.m
of public spaces and 9,000
parking places. Design:
Mecanoo in collaboration
with Autonome Forme,
Palermo
Competition Project: 2006,
second place
Client: Provincia Autonoma
di Trento
Structural Engineer: ABT
b.v., Delft
Mechanical and Electrical
Engineer: Peutz & Associés
B.V., Mook

Catholic Chapel of Sankt
Maria der Engelen
Nieuwe Crooswijkseweg
123, Rotterdam
(Netherlands)
Programme: Catholic chapel
of 120 sq.m built over the
remains of a nineteenth-
century chapel and design
of the public space
Design: 1998–99
Execution: 2000–01
Client: R.K. Begraafplaats
St. Laurentius, Rotterdam
General Contractor:
H&B bouw, Sassenheim
Structural Engineer:
ABT b.v., Delft
Building Costs Consultant:

Basalt Bouwadvies b.v., Nieuwegein
Artist: Mark Deconink

Visio, School for the Blind and Partially Sighted
Oud Bussummerweg 76, Huizen (Netherlands)
Programme: School of 3,015 sq.m for children with visual impairments and multiple handicaps with a gymnasium and therapeutic bath
Design: 2001–02
Execution: 2002–04
Client: Koninklijk Instituut tot Onderwijs van Slechtzienden en Blinden (KIOSB), Huizen
General Contractor: Klaassen Bouwmaatschappij Arnhem, Arnhem
Management Consultant: ICS/Deloitte & Touche, Amstelveen
Structural Engineer: Strackee b.v. Bouwadviesbureau, Amsterdam
Technical Engineer: DWA, Bodegraven
Acoustics Consultant: M+P Raadgevende Ingenieurs b.v., Aalsmeer

European Investment Bank
Boulevard Konrad Adenauer 100, Kirchberg Plateau, Luxembourg (Luxembourg)
Programme: Competition for the new headquarters of 66,000 sq.m
Competition Project: 2002, second place
Client: European Investment Bank, Luxembourg
Mechanical and Electrical Engineer: Buro Happold, Berlin/Glasgow

World Health Organisation-UNAIDS Headquarters
20 Avenue Appia, Geneva (Switzerland)
Programme: Competition for the new WHO-UNAIDS headquarters of 30,000 sq.m
Competition Project: 2002, first place
Client: OMS-ONUSIDA, Geneva

Landscape-Buildings and Buildings in the Landscape

Library of the Delft University of Technology
Prometheusplein 1, Delft (Netherlands)
Programme: University library of 15,000 sq.m with underground store for books, reading rooms, offices for the university publishing house, a room for the archives and for the consultation of rare books and exhibition area, study rooms, bookbinder's workshop and bookshop
Design: 1993–95
Execution: 1996–98
Client: ING Vastgoed, Ontwikkeling b.v, The Hague; TU Delft Vastgoedbeheer, Delft
General Contractor: Van Oorschot Versloot Bouw, Rotterdam; Boele van Eesteren V.O.F., Rotterdam; Scheldebouw architectural components, Middelburg for the façade
Structural Engineer: ABT b.v., Delft
Electrical Engineer: Deerns raadgevende ingenieurs b.v., Rijswijk
Plant Engineer: Ketel raadgevende ingenieurs b.v., Delft

Landscape: Van Ginkel b.v., Veenendaal

Office Villa Maliebaan
Maliebaan 16, Utrecht (Netherlands)
Programme: Underground extension and interior design of office-villa of 980 sq.m
Design: 1996–97
Execution: 1998–2000
Client: Andersson, Elffers, Felix, Utrecht
Agency: M.O.G. groep, Utrecht
General Contractor: Aannemersbedrijf Van Zoelen b.v., Utrecht; Bouwbedrijf M.J. de Nijs en Zn. b.v., Warmenhuizen
Structural Engineer: ABT b.v., Delft/Velp
Mechanical and Electrical Engineer: Valstar Simonis Raadgevende Ingenieurs, Rijswijk; Adviesbureau Hendriks b.v., Voorthuizen
Special Plant Engineer: Adviesbureau Peutz & Associes b.v., Zoetermeer
Artist: Linda Verkaaik
Landscape: Van Ginkel Veenendaal b.v., Veenendaal

Museum for Industry and Society Industrion
Kerkrade (Netherlands)
Programme: New museum for industry and craft in the mining and industrial area of Kerkrade
Design: 1993
Client: Museum voor Industrie en Samenleving

Philips Business Innovation Centre, FiftyTwoDegrees
Goffertpark, Nijmegen (Netherlands)
Programme: Multifunctional complex of 70,000 sq.m

with offices, a conference centre, catering, apartments, retail and sport facilities
Competition Project: 2004–05, first place
Execution: 2005–06
Client: Ballast Nedam Bouw, Arnhem; ICE Ontwikkeling, Nijmegen
General Contractor: Ballast Nedam Speciale Projecten, Utrecht
Structural Engineer: Adviesbureau Tielemans B.V., Nijmegen; ARUP, Amsterdam
Technical Engineer: Royal Haskoning, Nijmegen
Special Plant and Acoustic Engineer: Lichtveld Buis en Partners B.V., Nieuwegein
Mechanical Engineer: Burgers Ergon B.V, Eindhoven
Electrical Engineer: ETB Lubbers, Nijmegen
Fire Safety Consultant: DGMR Raadgevende Ingenieurs B.V., Arnhem
Traffic and Parking Consultant: Grontmij Parkconsult, Nijmegen

Learning Centre of the Ecole Polytechnique Fédérale de Lausanne
Campus École Polytechique Fédérale de Lausanne, Losanna (Switzerland)
Programme: Learning centre of 15,000 sq.m
Competition Project: 2004, second place
Client: École Polytechique Fédérale de Lausanne
Structural Engineer: ABT b.v., Delft/Velp
Technical Engineer: Deerns Raadgevende Ingenieurs b.v., Rijswijk

La Llotja Theatre and Conference Centre
Lérida (Spain)

Programme:
Theatre/conference centre
of 37,500 sq.m with two
conference halls (1,200
and 400 seats), the largest
of which also functions as
a theatre, a multifunctional
space and lounge
Competition Project:
2004–05, first place
Execution: 2006–08
Client: Gemeente Lérida;
Centre de Negocis i
de Convencions S.A.
Structural Engineer:
ABT b.v., Delft; BOMA,
Barcelona
Building Costs Consultant:
Basalt Nieuwegein;
Ardevols S.L. Barcelona
Technical Engineer: Deerns
Raadgevende Ingenieurs
b.v., Rijswijk; Einesa, Lérida
Acoustics Consultant:
Peutz b.v., Zoetermeer,
Higini Arau, Barcelona
Fire Safety Consultant:
Einesa, Lérida
Technical Consultants:
I-T Ardèvol i Associats S.L.,
Barcelona

Reuse and Conversion: Contrast as a Mark of Time

Cultural Centre and Museum
Deurne (Belgium)
Programme: Restoration
and extension of a cultural
centre with museum,
educational centre and
multifunctional spaces.
Design: 1994
Client: Gemeente Deurne

De Trust Theater
Kloveniersburgwal 50,
Amsterdam (Netherlands)
Programme: Conversion
of a former church into
a theatre of 2,700 sq.m

Design: 1995
Execution: 1996
Client: Toneelgroep
De Trust te Amsterdam
General Contractor:
Aannemingsmaatschappij
Konst en Van Polen b.v.,
Westwoud
Management Consultant:
J. van Rijs, Amsterdam
Structural Engineer:
ABT b.v., Delft
Special Plant Engineer:
Peutz & Associés b.v.,
Mook
Mechanical and Electrical
Engineer: Ketel
Raadgevende Ingenieurs,
Delft

Rozentheater
Rozengracht 117,
Amsterdam (Netherlands)
Programme: Renovation
of a theatre to become
a 2,100 sq.m youth centre
with a theatre hall (seating
190), a multifunctional hall
(seating fifty) and a bar
Design: 2001–03
Execution: 2004–05
Client: Bestuur Stichting
Rozentheater, Amsterdam
General Contractor:
Aannemingsmaatschappij
Konst en Van Polen,
Westwoud
Structural Engineer:
ABT b.v., Delft/Velp
Building Costs Consultant:
Basalt Bouwadvies,
Nieuwegein
Technical Engineer:
DHV AIB, Eindhoven
Acoustics Consultant:
DorsserBlesgraaf,
Eindhoven

Beurs – World Trade Center
Beursplein, Rotterdam
(Netherlands)
Programme: Interior
redesign of 11,000 sq.m

of the existing building with
a new entrance area, new
system of circulation, three
cafés/restaurants, offices,
conference rooms, shops,
day-care nursery and
garage for parking
Design: 2002–03
Execution: 2003–06
Client: Beurs Rotterdam
N.V., Rotterdam
General Contractor:
Van Omme & De Groot
b.v. Bouw-en
Aannemingsbedrijf,
Rotterdam
Structural Engineer:
DHV (D3BN), Rotterdam
Technical Engineer: De
Blaay-Van den Boogaard
Raadgevende Ingenieurs
b.v., Rotterdam

Territory in Movement

The Art of Engineering and the Aesthetics of Mobility
Programme: Project
on the motorway as design
resource from the
perspective of the road
user
Design: 1999
Client: Ministerie
van Verkeer en Waterstaat

Van Hasselt Junction
Van Hasseltlaan,
Amsterdam (Netherland)
Programme: Masterplan
for a multifunctional
program that includes
approximately 58,000
sq.m of apartments and
offices at an infrastructural
junction between the
North-South Line,
the IJ-Tunnel Route
and the main traffic link
to Amsterdam North
Design: 2001
Structural Engineer:

Van Rossum Raadgevende
Ingenieurs, Amsterdam
Technical Engineer: Advin,
Hoofddorp

Retailpark Westermaat Shopping Centre
Het Plein, Hengelo
(Netherland)
Programme: Urban plan
for a retail park with
an Ikea of 25,000 sq.m,
advertisement towers,
commercial space
of 25,000 sq.m
and a McDonald's
of 470 sq.m
Design: 1999–2002
Execution: 2001–04
Client: Ikea Beheer b.v.,
Amsterdam; TCN Property
Projects, Nieuwegein;
McDonald's Nederland
B.V., Amsterdam
General Contractor:
Van Wijnen Eibergen b.v.,
Eibergen; Bouwbedrijf
Wessels, Rijssel
Management Consultant:
Brink Groep Eindhoven
b.v., Eindhoven
Structural Engineer:
Aveco de Bondt;
Adviesbureau Duisters
b.v., Eindhoven
Electrical Engineer:
Jacobs projekten b.v.,
Breda; Halmos b.v.
Adviseurs, The Hague
Technical Engineer:
Scheepjens
Installatietechniek,
Den Bosch; Halmos b.v.
Adviseurs
Mechanical Engineer:
Jacobs projekten b.v.,
Breda; Halmos B.V.
Adviseurs, The Hague
Infrastructure Consultant:
Oranjewoud Bouw en
Vastgoed, Heerenveen
Fire Safety Consultant:
Adviesbureau Van Hooft
b.v., Rijkevoort

Hogeweld
Panamaplein 30,
The Hague (Netherland)
Programme: Multifunctional
complex of 13,500 sq.m
that includes two
elementary schools,
a multifunctional centre
of 1,500 sq.m, a sports hall
of 2,800 sq.m, a day-care
centre of 1,400 sq.m
and six apartments of 115
sq.m within the 'Hoge
Weld' urban plan
Design: 2000–02
Execution: 2003–04
Client: OCW vastgoed,
The Hague (scuole e centro
polifunzionale); HEVO
bouwmanagement, Den
Bosch (centro sportivo,
day-care, residenze)
Management: Deloitte
en Touche, Rotterdam;
HEVO Bouwmanagement,
Den Bosch
Structural Engineer:
Aronsohn Raadgevende
Ingenieurs b.v., Rotterdam
Mechanical and Electrical
Engineer: Valstar Simonis
Raadgevende Ingenieurs,
Rijswijk (scuole),
Hellebrekers, Nunspeet
(day-care, centro sportivo)
Special Plant Engineer:
Dorsserblesgraaf buro voor
bouwen & milieu b.v.,
The Hague (scuole), Peutz
en Associes Adviesbureau,
Mook (day-care,
centro sportivo)
Accountants: Basalt
Bouwadvies b.v.,
Nieuwegein

**Masterplan for
the Campus of Delft
University of Technology**
Mekelweg, Delft
(Netherland)
Programme: Masterplan
for the 60,000-sq.m
campus of the TU Delft.

Mecanoo in collaboration
with TU Delft Vastgoed
and ING Real Estate,
The Hague
Design: 2001–02 for
the masterplan, 2005
for Mekelpark
Client: College van Bestuur,
Technische Universiteit,
Delft

Annotated Bibliography

Not many monographs have been published on the work of Mecanoo, although a great deal has been written about the Delft-based studio in architecture magazines. Here we will mention: Kees Somer, *Mecanoo*, 010 Publishers, Rotterdam 1995; published in English translation by John Kirkpatrick as *Mecanoo – Architecture*, 010 Publishers, Rotterdam 1996. This was the first monograph on Mecanoo, with an interesting introductory essay that explains the origin of the studio's work in the course of Design Analysis at the Delft University of Technology. Annette Le Cuyer, *Mecanoo*, Michigan Architecture Papers, Ann Arbor 1999. This presents a selection of twelve works realized by the studio and includes Henk Döll's essay, "The Reflective Architect," written for a symposium in memory of Donald Schon held at the Delft University of Technology on 23 January 1998. Federico Bilò, *Mecanoo*, Edilstampa Editrice dell'ANCE, Rome 2003. The first monograph in Italian, it too presents twelve of the studio's works, focusing primarily on works of public architecture.

More exhaustive are the books published by members of the studio itself. In particular: Francine Houben/Mecanoo Architecten, *Compositie Contrast Complexiteit*, NAi Publishers, Rotterdam 2001. Also published in English under the title *Composition Contrast Complexity*, Birkhäuser, Basel-Boston-Berlin 2001. Houben's book presents a forthright picture of Mecanoo's method of design through an account of the studio's principal works. More specific are the following books on individual buildings and projects: Mecanoo Architecten, *Bibliotheek Technische Universiteit Delft*, 010 Publishers, Rotterdam 2000. Mecanoo Architecten, *TU Delft Masterplan*, Delft University Press, Delft 2002. It is also worth citing the catalogue of the first Rotterdam Architecture Biennial directed by Francine Houben (ed.), *Mobility: A Room with a View*, NAi Publishers, Rotterdam 2003.

Mecanoo is covered in several books on Dutch architecture that compare the work of the studio in Delft with that of other contemporary planners and architects. The most important are: Hans Ibelings, *The Artificial Landscape, Contemporary Architecture, Urbanism and Landscape Architecture in the Netherlands*, NAi Publishers, Rotterdam 2002. It contains an anthology of critical writings including Roemer van Toorn, "Fresh Conservatism and Beyond," originally published in *Archis*, 11, 1997.

Bart Lootsma, *Superdutch. New Architecture in the Netherlands*, Thames & Hudson, London 2000. This is the most widely read text on the new Dutch architecture at an international level.

The relationship of contemporary Dutch architecture with the Modern movement and with functionalism is discussed in a pamphlet and in a historical analysis, both by Hans Ibelings: Hans Ibelings, *Dutch Architecture in the Twentieth Century*, NAi Publishers, Rotterdam 1994; Hans Ibelings, *Supermodernism, Architecture in the Age of Globalization*, NAi Publishers, Rotterdam 2002; Hans Ibelings, *Twentieth Century Urban Planning in the Netherlands*, NAi Publishers, Rotterdam 1999. Then it is worth mentioning the work of the Crimson group of young historians, based in Rotterdam, who have demolished the myths of Dutch functionalism in: Crimson, *Too Blessed to be Depressed, Crimson Architectural Historians 1994-2002*, NAi Publishers 2002.

The theme of housing in contemporary Dutch architecture is dealt with in: Arjen Oosterman, *Housing in the Netherlands, Exemplary Architecture in the Nineties*, NAi Publishers 1996, which compares the works of Mecanoo with other recent housing complexes.

The themes of tectonics and materiality in the work of Mecanoo and other contemporary architects are discussed in: Annette Le Cuyer, *Radical Tectonics, Enric Miralles, Günther Behnisch, Mecanoo, Patkau Architects*, Thames & Hudson, London 2001.

The question of the post-medium world and the investigation of themes and ideas in parallel means of expression is linked to the development of the contemporary arts and in particular the Conceptual movement in the seventies and eighties. It is dealt with exhaustively in: Rosalind Krauss, *A Voyage on the North Sea: Art in the Age of the Post-Medium Condition*, Thames & Hudson, London 1999.

As well as in the aforementioned *The Artificial Landscape*, the relationship of Dutch culture with the landscape and with diagrammatic representation is examined from the historical perspective in: Svetlana Alpers, *The Art of Describing, Dutch Painting in the Seventeenth Century*, Chicago University Press, Chicago 1983.

Photograph Credits

All rendering, plans and sections
are by Mecanoo Architecten;
all photographs are by Christian
Richters.